The Baroque

LITERATURE

AND CULTURE

IN SEVENTEENTH-CENTURY

EUROPE

PETER N. SKRINE

The Baroque

LITERATURE

AND CULTURE

IN SEVENTEENTH-CENTURY

EUROPE

Methuen & Co Ltd

First published in 1978
by Methuen & Co Ltd
11 New Fetter Lane London EC4P 4EE
© 1978 Peter N. Skrine
Printed in Great Britain
at the University Printing House
Cambridge

ISBN 0 416 56290 6 (hardback)
ISBN 0 416 56300 7 (paperback)

Contents

Introduction

Can any cultural movement be explained? The one now called *baroque* dominated most of Western Europe from the late sixteenth century to the 1720s. During that long time it went through various phases, affecting some arts, some countries more than others; to readers of this book that will become clear.

What is the baroque? There are many overlapping definitions. To many who have written well about it, it means a mode of European painting; a style of architecture; a cultural phenomenon which manifested itself most noticeably in the fine and applied arts. To others, the baroque means an attitude to life which arose after the Renaissance and the Protestant Reformation, and found expression in music, literature and painting. In countries where it has left strong and evident traces there is a natural tendency to rate it highly and to describe the finest and most representative products of the seventeenth century as baroque, without further definition. This is particularly the case in Italy and Spain, in Austria and Germany. In England, however, as in France, there is a deeply ingrained and understandable reluctance to accept the term. Not only have both these Western nations been much less marked by baroque visual art; they are also apt to remember its originally pejorative meaning, more suitable for describing foreign achievements than their own. In general, Protestant countries share this reluctance, and tend to regard the baroque as Roman Catholic. The case of France, however, reveals how complex the situation really is.

The baroque developed at different speeds in different places, affecting different areas of art and culture, and coalescing more or less with indigenous traditions. Yet it was by nature cosmopolitan and, like the élite who encouraged and enjoyed it, travelled more readily and widely than we today might think. Though Italy played a large part in its emergence and radiation, should its sources be located there alone? There are arguments for seeing it as an almost spontaneous expression of a state of mind and attitude to the world which permeated seventeenth-century Europe and had its simultaneous counterparts in other, distant places: not only Spanish Mexico and Portuguese Brazil, but the Persia of Shah Abbas, and even Japan.

But let us stay in Christian Western Europe. There the rise of two significant phenomena were perhaps more responsible for the baroque's emergence than any other factors: the concept of absolutist monarchy and the theatrical stage. Europe had not enjoyed either on such a scale since the fall of the ancient Roman Empire. When absolutism and the theatre came together in royal command performances in seventeenth-century palaces, the baroque was more in evidence than elsewhere — except in the Roman Catholic church, whose monolithic claims and sense of occasion made it a patron of baroque artists everywhere.

Hence the importance of drama, royal prestige and spiritual values in this account of Europe's baroque culture. In so far as it is intended for the English-speaking reader, the relative closeness and, of course, remoteness of the examples cited has been very much taken into account. French instances are thus far more in evidence than the topic would seem at first to justify, while references and allusions to Spain, Germany and Holland are by comparison relatively few, despite the literary and artistic richness of these nations. Yet they *are* mentioned more often than is usually the case, and connections are drawn which may surprise and interest those who know their seventeenth-century history but, through no fault of their own, cannot understand the major European tongues which, in their different ways, all forged their own dialect of the common baroque cultural and artistic language.

Connections, analogies and counterparts: these are more telling than arid facts and vague hypotheses. So abstract generalizations are played down in favour of a more thematic presentation relaxed enough to pause for exploration, yet swift enough not to lose the wood for the trees. It does, however, emerge that the decade on either side of 1660 saw the zenith of the baroque in Europe — a cultural climax prepared for by the 1620s and 1630s, and echoed by the late baroque achievements of the early eighteenth century. The reasons for this cultural pattern are several, and they form a recurring theme in the eight chapters. These concentrate on various interdependent facets of baroque culture as seen from the vantage point which literature provides by virtue of the fact that it articulates the notions underlying the music, art and architecture of the times when it was written. Literature is written to be read by those who actively or passively create the tastes and fashions of a period. This was especially true of the playwrights and theatregoers of the baroque period. Success, applause, an appreciative public: stage plays need these far more than paintings or poetry. Thus they can help us to recapture the feel and atmosphere of baroque Europe.

Each chapter focuses on one of the eight areas where the baroque expressed itself most successfully. And each presents a separate exploration of different, interlinked facets of a vast and maze-like subject. Quotations, when not given in the original, are paraphrases or personal translations, except when they are given in English versions current at the time and thus conveying the flavour of the period. Footnotes do not appear. The text is self-sufficient, though wider reading is naturally encouraged.

I

'*All the world's a stage*'

A pervasive image captures the baroque age's view of man's condition and its love of the theatrical: 'All the world's a stage'. To the English-speaker this image obviously sounds Shakespearian, and it would be ridiculous not to realize that Shakespeare's creative imagination, the richest at work as the seventeenth century opened, contains elements and features that anticipate the baroque, and link it with the culture of the Elizabethan age in England. No period arises unheralded in time, and all European literary and artistic phases can be seen as little more than a rearrangement of the pre-existent pieces of the complex mosaic of Western culture.

> All the world's a stage,
> And all the men and women merely players:
> They have their exits and their entrances . . .

There is a convincingly English and Shakespearian ring about Jaques's famous lines from *As You Like It* (performed in 1599, though not published until 1623). But the notion they express is one that can be found all over Europe during that period between 1600 and 1700 which has become familiar to most modern European poetry-readers, concert-goers and art-lovers as the Baroque Age. Not that one should promptly fall into the over-simplifying temptation of equating the term 'baroque' with the seventeenth century as a whole. Much of that century's art, its poetry and its thinking was far from baroque, and many a seventeenth-century person must have viewed what the term today describes with grave misgiving and even, perhaps, as the work of the devil. There is certainly nothing baroque about the sober mansion of an English country gentleman of the mid-seventeenth century, or the town house of a Dutch merchant; and there was as little of it about the churches where they worshipped as in the realistic, pragmatic attitude to life which underlay their sense of balance and their plain prosperity. It was a century that saw the fulfilment of a Protestant lifestyle in many parts of Northern Europe; which saw, too, the rise of scientific inquiry, and of the rationalist philosophy associated with Descartes. And none of these characteristic seventeenth-century phenomena in any way claims the description 'baroque' — indeed they are in their different ways fundamentally opposed to it. The origins of the baroque, like those of the image of the world as a stage which it made so particularly its own, go back to distant periods and obscure, sometimes unlikely sources, and to trace that image back is in many ways to lay bare some of the essential impulses that anticipated and helped to form it. For only at times that shared something of the same view of the world could such a simile come to mind.

It had been given its best-known and most eloquent modern expression in Erasmus' neo-Latin masterpiece, *The Praise of Folly* (1509), an English translation of which appeared in 1668:

> If any one seeing a Player acting his Part on a Stage, should go about to strip him of his disguise, and shew him to the people in his true Native Form, would he not, think ye, not onely spoil the whole design of the Play, but deserve himself to be pelted off with stones, as a Phantastical Fool, and one out of his wits? But Nothing is more common with them, than such changes. The same person, one while personating a Woman, and another while, a Man; now a Youngster, and by and by, a grim Seigniour; now a King, and presently a Peasant; now a God, and in a trice agen, an ordinary Fellow; But to discover this, were to spoil all, it being the onely thing that entertains the Eyes of the Spectators: And what is all this Life but a kind of Comedy, wherein men walk up and down in one another's Disguises, and Act their respective Parts, till the property-man brings 'em back to the Tyring House: And yet, he often orders a different Dress, and makes him, that came but just off, in the

robes of a King, put on the Raggs of a Beggar: Thus are all things represented by counterfeit, and yet without this, there were no living.

The greatest of Europe's Renaissance humanists in relaxed and intimate mood finds himself touching here on a rich complexity of themes which are generally associated with the baroque. That of illusion and reality is central to the passage, but accompanied by intimations of the fickleness of fortune, the vanity of all earthly pomp, and the absolute supremacy of the divine. But it would be unwise not to remember that the passage is taken from the humorously ironic speech which Erasmus put into the mouth of Folly, a speech in which that much-maligned goddess attempts to justify herself by a shrewd and far-sweeping survey of human actions and aspirations. Erasmus was no fool: so would he share her views? He was also very deeply versed in the cultural and moral heritage of classical antiquity, to the restoration of which he devoted the labours of a lifetime, and was well aware that this effective passage on the theme of the world as a stage was taken from a dialogue by the late Hellenistic Greek satirist Lucian of Samosata. In his dialogue *Necromancy*, which concerns an imaginary visit to the underworld by Menippus, a Cynic philosopher, the traveller returned from those infernal regions says that what he saw there made him think that human life is like a play or pageant written by a poet, in which each player is given his allotted role. They may change their condition in the course of the play; but when the play is over each becomes what he was before. Only the fool will wish that the play might go on for ever, and forget that the costume he wore was only borrowed. For such is the way of the world.

It is well known that, in the centuries which produced the Renaissance and followed it, the revival of classical studies fostered a general interest in Greek and Roman antiquity. By and large, the interest of the fifteenth and sixteenth centuries had concentrated on the 'classical' heritage of antiquity — on those works and systems of thought that provided a norm and criterion for human taste and conduct regardless of time and place. In Italy and elsewhere the influence of Aristotle had given way to that of Plato, for Aristotle had dominated the now-receding Middle Ages, while Cicero and Horace became the models for educated writers

throughout Europe, and Virgil and Homer the subjects of learned
theorizing on the nature of the epic, or heroic poem. But the
classical canon as we still know it today having been at last firmly
established, there became evident signs of restlessness with it.
While continuing to pay all due respect to the aesthetic and moral
pre-eminence of the major classical writers, people started in many
places gradually to turn towards the less obvious, and to develop a
fondness for the byways of the ancient world. This did not only
mean a delving into the arcana of ancient mysteries and esoteric
philosophies. Sometimes it also meant a return to some of those
ancient writers whose fantastic and incredible worlds had delighted
readers many hundreds of years before and whose fame had in some
cases been considerable before the Renaissance had even really
begun. None was to exert so deep and far-reaching an influence on
the shaping of baroque taste as the late Greek writer Heliodorus,
whose vast romance *Aethiopica* (*c*. A D 232-50), the story of the
loves and adventures of Theagenes and Chariclea, was to provide
the basic model for the plots, style and narrative techniques of all
the romances that proliferated in seventeenth-century Europe, and
which, like their ancient model, delighted in the violent separation
of tender young lovers, the encapsulation of flashbacks in an
exciting, forward-moving action, the suspense generated by
frequent unforeseen reversals and dire threats to life and chastity,
and by frequent recourse to disguise, all in a Mediterranean setting
and embellished with sophisticated dialogues and passages of
ornate description. Nor had the Roman philosopher and dramatist
Seneca, unfortunate tutor to the emergent monster Nero, ever been
entirely forgotten. He had always been one of the central strands of
the European tradition; but now, in the late Renaissance or early
baroque period from, say, 1575 onwards, his return to popularity
and esteem both on the stage and in the library of every thoughtful
person was symptomatic of impending changes. Notions of an
ordered world, of a comprehensible cosmos, and a human nature
constant, rounded and self-contained were giving way to sensations
of impending confusion, and to the awareness of a universe vaster
and more complex and a human psychology less typecast, more
passionate and variable than had been imagined. Senecan philosophy, with its stoical concentration on the ideal of self-stability in
the flux and chaos of surrounding life; Senecan drama, with its
outrageous actions, grandiloquent protagonists and monitory

choruses: these now enjoyed a marked return to favour exemplified by the cosmopolitan intellectual success of *De Constantia* (1584), written by the Flemish neo-Senecan thinker, Justus Lipsius, with its apposite and judicious blend of ancient philosophy and post-Reformation Christianity.

Seneca, playwright and philosopher, was bound to appeal more than ever before to the new age. His particular version of traditional Greek stoicism, with its insistence on the need for tranquillity of mind and constancy of purpose in a shifting and perilous world; his larger-than-life, high-flown dramatic adaptations of the tragic themes and subjects of ancient Greece; but above all, his personal attempt to reconcile both aspects of his career in the setting of Nero's Rome, that golden Rome of unsurpassed splendour and cold-blooded intrigue so laconically described in the *Annals* of Tacitus: all three of these factors recommended him to the age which was to witness the successful completion of St Peter's Basilica and the construction (from 1656 on) of Bernini's masterstroke — the colonnades that open up before it to draw the overawed visitor into the embrace of Holy Church. Confidently Christian these edifices might be, yet they also seemed to be a triumphant resurrection of the vanished Rome which Tacitus recorded, and in which Seneca developed his philosophy of prudence and fortitude and wrote his violent, often beautiful plays before being driven by his tyrant master to commit the memorable suicide that Monteverdi was to evoke with all the lyric power of new-found operatic form in his *L'Incoronazione di Poppea* (1642).

Were those Latin plays performed? In fact it isn't certain. But to the baroque era, unlike the Renaissance, the idea of closet drama, perfect on the printed page but never to be translated into the reality of stage performance, was something sterile and irrelevant. What the ancients might or might not have done was now at last to be fully realized: on the vestiges and foundations of their earlier achievement a new European culture would be built which would vie with the most splendid epochs of the past and rival the beauty and grandeur of imperial Rome, its most admired forerunner. It was a cultural ambition which in all major Western European countries put the finishing touch to the progress of their respective languages — Italian, French, Spanish, Portuguese, English, Dutch, German — towards literary maturity and national prestige, objectives which often manifested themselves in the paradoxical yet compulsive desire to imitate the ancients and even to outdo them. Thus in France and the Netherlands especially, the rise of a vernacular drama illustrating the theme of the *theatrum mundi* was by many seen as a deliberate attempt to re-create both the spirit and the outward form and appearance of ancient drama. For both monarchical France and republican Holland, each rising in economical and political terms after its vicissitudes during the later sixteenth century, shared at least this: both felt a deep nostalgia for the virtues and greatness of ancient Rome and sought inspiration in its history and in the thoughts and writings of its poets. To Vondel (1587-1679), Holland's outstanding baroque writer, Rome could indeed be ' 's werelds hooft', the world's head, in its dual capacities as the greatest pagan civilization and as the nerve-centre of Christian tradition. But it was the French dramatist Pierre Corneille (1606-84) who formulated the eternal, universal presence of Rome and its multiple influences most strikingly in one of the many fine plays which gave modern France the 'Roman' drama which the Eternal City had probably never enjoyed: 'Rome n'est plus dans Rome, elle est toute où je suis' (*Sertorius*, 1662).

And there is a certain truth in this confident claim. Wherever the baroque spirit manifested itself in stone, on canvas, or in words, Rome rose again. It did so not only by coming apparently to life again in the rhetorical tirades and debates of plays based on some episode or other from the history, often enough, of later imperial Rome: plays concerned with the fate of emperors or the tribulations of their often Christian victims. The Roman ideal was also radiated by books of enormous influence at the time, such as *Le Romain*, an essay published by the elegantly thought-provoking French writer Guez de Balzac in 1644 and advocating the 'Roman' qualities of virtue and duty, on which true magnanimity and glory, attributes beloved of the period, are shown to be based.

Now certainly, ever-present though it was, the old Rome of the emperors had passed away, an example to posterity, maybe, of what the human being is capable of, yet, like the Forum and Imperial Baths, an impressive reminder, too, of the impermanence of all monuments, all achievements, even the most solid. But alongside its ruins, visited by many a baroque artist and writer, and surrounded in those days by scenes of rustic indifference, with cattle grazing and shepherd boys playing, indeed right in the midst of them was rising a new Rome whose formative influence on the emergence and shaping of baroque art, architecture and music was to prove immense. Enhancing the already legendary splendours of Renaissance Rome, like Michelangelo's dome for St Peter's and the rooms painted by Raphael inside the Vatican, Pope Paul V Borghese (1605-21) and his architect Carlo Maderna completed the mighty building, while his highly cultured successor, Urban VIII Barberini (1623-44), encouraged the supreme genius of baroque sculpture and architecture, Gian Lorenzo Bernini (1598-1680), to erect the astonishing baldacchino over its high altar: the great colonnades that lead up to the church were to come later, commissioned by the third great art-loving pope of the baroque period, Alexander VII Chigi (1655-67), sworn enemy and rival of Louis XIV of France at a time when competition between the European princes for cultural prestige and imperial glory was at its height. But it was in a different part of the city — in a Roman square, the Piazza Navona, once the site of the stadium built by Nero in which many Christians were said to have met a violent end and which had now become the social hub of Roman life — that the new baroque Rome achieved its greatest triumph. For here one of Bernini's most breathtakingly ornamental fountains, that of the Four Rivers (1651), was in 1652-3 set against the spectacular backdrop of the Church of St Agnes, masterpiece of Italy's other major baroque architect, Francesco Borromini (1599-1667). No Roman emperor, not even the vainglorious art-lover Nero, could surely ever have imagined what splendours would be generated by this Roman encounter between the art of antiquity and the modern imagination.

Pagan pomp and Christian purpose meet and fuse in the Piazza Navona, making it an epitome of the baroque, and the theatrical quality so evident in it provides a key to the age. Not only was this square the showpiece of contemporary Rome and the scene for countless entertainments which even included artificial inundation and subsequent mock-heroic sea battles. The vast, curving façade of the church, and the oval square before it, were themselves a stage on which the secular nobility and the dignitaries of the church could play their several parts, conscious, as baroque man always was, that the eyes of others were upon them, that they were being watched. But to the baroque person this sensation did not lead to selfconsciousness in the modern, post-Romantic sense. It fostered, rather, a sense of self-esteem, of proud complacency even: an

awareness of the immense importance of cutting a figure in the
world, of projecting an image as meaningful and deliberate as any
conveyed by the painting and sculpture of the day. The baroque
age's art, like its stage performances, was by no means as unrealistic
to its contemporaries as it now perhaps may seem to us.

Thus it was that the image of the world as a stage could at the
height of the baroque cultural period in Europe be elaborated into
a full and valid view of life. This was the case in the remarkable
verse dedication prefaced by the German dramatist Daniel Casper
von Lohenstein (1635-83) to the published text of his high-
baroque tragedy *Sophonisbe* (1680), first performed in 1666 to
celebrate the marriage between the Holy Roman Emperor Leopold I
and the Infanta Margarita Teresa of Spain (1651-73), younger
stepsister of Louis XIV's queen, and daughter of that Philip IV so
often portrayed by Velázquez. Basing himself on the modest
statement 'I offer but a play', Lohenstein in this 276-line poem
develops the theme of 'play' (= *Spiel*) in a virtuoso set of variations
which represent this theme's most extended and elaborate deployment in baroque Europe. Everything here is involved in restless,
ever-changing activity, from the stars in their cosmic zodiacal
patterns, and the elements playing in sky, sea and earth, to the
gaudy caterpillar and the playful dolphin; but, above all, man, vain
plaything of time and chance, is the eternal player for ever making
the world his toy:

> Für allen aber ist der Mensch ein Spiel der Zeit:
> Das Glücke spielt mit ihm / und er mit allen Sachen.

The games and gambols of man's childhood become the sports of
youth, and these the acts and gambles of maturity. Love's comedy
is acted out, all reasonable balance is lost — yet there's not a play
that isn't dominated by it, for the interplay of love, reason and
ambition can be truly tragic, and tragedy makes the finest play. The
theatre glows with ivory, gold and silk as Nero, imperial actor, plays
his part. And who sees more of the performance than the
nobleman who has chosen to make the court the scene for his own
act? He may start out as favourite of a prince, but by the evening
the hollow plot will be acted out: raise the final curtain when the
play is done and you may find a maggot-eaten corpse still clothed in
fading purple. But Rome turned funerals into spectacles and
pageants; it laughed to see the gladiator fall, and erected statues to

men who played their life's part well. And, like Athens before it, the Imperial City thought nothing of squandering whole fortunes on the show.

The way the basic image is developed in Lohenstein's Dedication to *Sophonisbe* is significant, and makes the poem a document of major cultural importance. The notion of *theatrum mundi*, of 'all the world's a stage', has been expanded to embrace the whole of life: all nature, the entire cosmos, all created things are involved in it. The bounds of conventional metaphor have burst to open up a universal dimension — a natural and eternal backcloth against which Lohenstein can proceed to develop an interpretation of the concepts of play, stage and actor which represents a peculiarly baroque view of human motivation and human achievement. For the psychology of the individual and the workings of society are, like the culture they have in common, seen in terms at once of play-acting and make-believe and yet also of a deeper and more dramatic existential necessity. The microcosm that is man, from the moment of his conception caught up in his role and act, yet always more or less aware that he is only acting his role, is seen by the German poet as a reflection here below of activities on an altogether vaster and more sublime plane — the restless, compulsive interplay of elemental forces on an infinite and cosmic scale. And it is this that endows puny man with an element at least of nobility. The gold and purple he likes to strut about in may only be worthless fustian; but the parts he plays are scripted by God the Creator. Their re-enactment on the stage must therefore surely be the truest way of illustrating and conveying the meaning of the world. Truth is mirrored in the make-believe.

Most cultured European men and women would have agreed with the views advanced by this well-read and sophisticated German, though many might have found them altogether too profane, too compounded with the vestiges and echoes of pagan classical thinking, to be fully acceptable; too little concerned with man's transcendental part, and the salvation of his soul. And most would have shared Lohenstein's fondness for the stage, just as they would also have known how to appreciate the inexhaustible command of conceit and pun with which he generates and sustains his argument in favour of the theatre as a vital part of human life and culture. But in Britain the recent and shortlived attempt by Cromwell's republican government to close the playhouses and put

a stop to such theatrical enthusiasm had proved a bold if vain effort
to hold back the tide of baroque culture and dampen its appeal.
Republican Holland had taken a rather different approach, and had
done so with a sound good sense which was to help account for what
might seem a very paradoxical phenomenon — the fact that the
major dramatist and poet of this staunchly Calvinist society became
a fervent Roman Catholic. But though they were far removed from
the ornate and Italianate extravagance of Rome and those more
northerly cultural centres that were attempting to emulate it, the
Dutch did share something of the rest of Europe's love of the
theatre. This they revealed when in 1638 the City Fathers of
Amsterdam attended the official opening of their municipal
playhouse or Schouwburg, a theatre of very up-to-date design
which employed a troupe of twenty-four salaried actors and
actresses, as well as producers, musicians and six officially
appointed 'regents' or managers: an establishment soon to become
the envy of foreign visitors. Over its front entrance was inscribed a
couplet by that poet, Vondel:

> De wereld is een speeltoneel,
> Elk speelt zijn rol en krijgt zijn deel

'The world's a stage, each plays his role and gets his share.' The
notion was indeed ubiquitous.

Amsterdam in the 1630s was a town of growing prestige and
commercial affluence with, like its Italian counterpart Venice, a
population of some 140,000. Vastly different though their
temperaments, traditions and morals were, both cities shared a
high degree of civic and republican pride, were built on the water
over which their exotic riches came, and attached great value to
theatrical entertainments of a high standard. Their self-esteem as
well as their appreciation of a good aesthetic investment were
reflected too in the innumerable paintings and portraits commissioned by their wealthier citizens. And both enjoyed the working
presence of great artists who, between them, show something of the
range of visual baroque art: in Venice, Veronese (*c.* 1528-88)
whose large-scale opulence and rich colour exerted great influence
on that art's emergence, and in Amsterdam Rembrandt (1606-69)
and Ruisdael (1628/9-82), who between them display something
of the range of Dutch painting in the seventeenth century, and its
ability to convey spiritual intensity, erotic delight and pastoral

tranquillity. But Venice's greatest painters — Veronese, Titian, Tintoretto — were forerunners rather than exponents of the baroque, and it was from the theatre that its truly baroque achievement radiated far and wide. It was a theatre associated with mime and gesture, mask and masquerade, with comedy and tragicomedy, and with the dramatic power and melodic richness of its vast and colourful operatic entertainments provided for its luxury-loving audiences by Monteverdi (1567-1643) and Cavalli (1602-76). Amsterdam could produce no counterpart to this, any more than London could, and for the greater part of the baroque age the Italians and especially the Venetians were to remain unequalled in the sphere of theatrical music and lyric drama. In Protestant Holland it was the word that reigned supreme upon the stage, as in its churches. There — quite the opposite of England's major mid-century poet, Milton, who avoided the stage, broke with tradition and directed English poetry away from the playhouse towards a vast and epic theatre of the imagination — Holland's main seventeenth-century writer, Vondel, chose the stage as his predominant medium, and roused the imaginations of his fellow countrymen with an impressive sequence of tragic dramas produced between 1610 and 1667: dates that span the years from Shakespeare's maturity to the drama of the Restoration. Thus in different ways the two great maritime and trading cities of Amsterdam and Venice had some contribution of importance to make to the evolution and expression of that deep sense of the theatrical with which baroque Europe and its culture were permeated. Venice expressed that sense in primarily musical terms: in music that could move and delight its audiences with alternate ease, and which also required an exquisite and often prolific variety of settings to set it off and gladden eyes that were used to the finest painting. Amsterdam, for its part, could merely claim to have established a well-run theatre in the same season as Venice opened the first opera house in Europe, the Teatro di San Cassiano (1637/8). But that Dutch theatre was the imaginative home of a man of extraordinary creative range, who cast the conflicts which he felt, saw and dreamt of into large-scale dramas, monumental and static in form, yet each endowed with its own explosive force and lyric eloquence.

The United Provinces of the Netherlands, of which Holland was but one, had achieved their independence from Spain in the truce of 1609, and their formal political recognition by the Treaty of

Münster in 1648 at the end of the Thirty Years War. Little might seem to link two such arch-enemies, so different in their religious attitudes, their moral and social values, and their immediate destinies. Yet in Spain, too, the notion of 'all the world's a stage' had been translated into a national zest for stage performances, with the result that Spanish literature in Spain's Golden Age is largely, if not solely, of the dramatic kind. The cloak-and-dagger world of Spanish drama was to provide a major source of European pleasure in the baroque period: indeed Spain's contribution to the swagger and panache, the reckless valour, dash and darker side of many a European work of the seventeenth century, was quite as significant as the contribution it made to the conventions of court etiquette and personal behaviour, conventions that exerted an influence at once stifling and stimulating on the lifestyle of the age, a lifestyle which was at once their fulfilment and a reaction to them. Spain's political, economic and social hegemony at the outset of the period was immense, even if it was disputed here and there by the English, Dutch and French. Yet, curiously, its impact on baroque culture in Europe was in some ways far less great than its prestige suggests. The impact of the role it played in the New World was quite another matter.

In Calderón, as in Vondel, the baroque attained new heights. For church and court alike Calderón (1600-81) wrote his plays. Some were fantastic allegorical extravaganzas of the utmost splendour for the gardens of Buen Retiro, the country palace which King Philip IV then favoured, like *El mayor encanto amor* ('Love's the greatest enchantment'), a highly wrought depiction of the struggle waged for Ulysses' heart between Virtue and the seductress Circe, with ships and nymphs afloat around an enchanted island, and with Philip IV (1605-65) an appreciative spectator, soon to build his splendid theatre there, known as the Coliseo and boasting the most advanced theatrical machinery and illusionistic devices in Europe. The pomp and spectacle favoured at court had their sacred and more popular counterpart in the Corpus Christi plays — the *autos sacramentales* — which by 1600 had become very much a speciality of Spain, and of which Calderón was to be the most imaginative and impressive exponent, especially in his *El gran teatro del mundo* (*c.* 1641, published 1655), the play which was to give the image of the world as a stage its supreme and most strikingly baroque interpretation. For here God is Himself the author of the play produced on the stage of the world when the curtain of chaos has risen, and acted extempore by those to whom its parts are given. The post-mortem on their performance is an instance of sublime irony at the expense of all our criticism; for few have really acted well, however well their parts may have been acted. Meanwhile the play-within-a-play in which they have been acting is judged in the last instance by criteria that are deadly earnest — gone is our earlier flippancy. What starts off as a conceit dramatized, a familiar metaphor embellished, ends up an act of sacramental faith, a glorious anthem in praise of piety, a grandiose allegory of revealed religion.

Of course the figures in Calderón's spiritual allegory of the *theatrum mundi* are stereotypes. Ambitious king and beautiful woman, overworked peasant and bullied beggar, complacent rich man and wise priest, they are in themselves allegories, embodiments of stock characteristics, yet they are all so realistically caught up in the very act of living that they do not know it. And as allegorical figures organized into a symbolic theatrical display, they have a spiritual function to perform as well as a dramatic one. Of course their performances turn out to be less perfect than the Lord had hoped: Divine Grace, as prompter, has a thankless task with such all-too-human material. But fortunately the Lord is also an indulgent spectator. When, at the end, He decides to invite all — all save the rich man — to His celestial table there to partake of His sacramental supper, and the sacred elements of the Eucharist actually appear as properties on the stage, Calderón is emphatically and fervently upholding the Faith by holding up to his public a symbolic representation of its inner meaning and message. This is no mere baroque ostentation; rather it is a truly baroque ostension, in which words and action, monstrance-like, show forth the radiant mystery of the Christian and Catholic faith. The climax of the play, like some massive, ardent Spanish altarpiece of the period, imparts to its spectator something of the timeless majesty of the central Christian drama — Christ's sacrifice and man's redemption — as seen through post-Reformation Roman Catholic eyes.

Calderón's *El gran teatro del mundo* is one of those instances — and there are many — when baroque art and literature triumphantly succeeded in embodying that Christian philosophy infused with classical pagan ideas which had in the first place brought the baroque into being. That these instances can also sometimes even seem to express basic human insight is but a measure of that achievement, or perhaps the confirmation of its abiding validity. The style and mood may be quite patently different, yet there is a real affinity between that Spanish sacred action and Milton's audacious epic, just as there is more than a mere similarity of timing between those works of the creative poetic imagination and Rome's Piazza Navona, that setting for man's ephemeral entertainments against a backdrop of eternity given form and outline in the shape of Borromini's dome, towers and columns. All three affirm the world, its joys, its shapes, its colour; yet they imply with massive, forceful eloquence, as only the baroque could, that there is more, far more besides, and that these are really nothing, less than nothing. The play is all; yet how soon a play is over. It was a striking symbol, and it provides a key for our understanding of an age.

Common though the notion of 'all the world's a stage' was to the baroque mind and imagination all over Europe, the actual evolution of its theatrical traditions was in fact extremely varied. In Spain the development was as seemingly natural, smooth and irresistible as was that country's rise to pre-eminence in the politics and commerce of the world, and it was to last until gradual decline set in in this sphere too during the latter part of the seventeenth century. By 1600 playhouses were numerous throughout the country. Called *corrales*, they were originally and usually sponsored by hospitals and charities, and were in fact the courtyards located in the centre of blocks of town houses. Quite literally, here the theatre was the world; and its social function and importance were fully recognized by the civic authorities which increasingly stepped in to lend it their support. In this respect at least, the Netherlands learnt something from Spain and from Madrid's two famous playhouses, the Corral del Principe and the Corral de la Cruz, rather than from France or England, where the rise of the theatre and its seventeenth-century evolution was less closely and consciously linked to the needs and thinking of church and state. For here the position was very different. In both countries the smooth and logical unfolding of seventeenth-century culture was interrupted or at least disturbed by the social, political and religious upheavals of that period of disorientation, restlessness and malaise which marked the middle years of the century. In England a glorious theatrical tradition was disrupted by the uncongenial atmosphere and hostile attitudes of Civil War and Commonwealth, which brought to the fore outlooks and ideologies profoundly at variance with the ethos of the baroque. In 1642 the London theatres closed: this dramatic interregnum was to last until the Restoration of the Monarchy in 1660. What had preceded the closure was the final flowering of England's in- digenous Elizabethan and Jacobean dramatic and cultural tradition, an insular development which sometimes — as in some of the more artificially contrived and elegant romances and tragicomedies of Beaumont and, especially, Fletcher — looked forward, or abroad, towards a conception of stage illusion and its metaphorical poten- tial at least as much baroque as it was Shakespearian. But it was only with the return of king and nobility in 1660 that England suddenly and with an upsurge of dramatic activity established a type of theatre that does indeed reflect continental Europe's baroque obsession with the underlying theatricality of life. Whereas Elizabethan London had enjoyed the attraction of numerous playhouses, with the new, more baroque approach to stage enter- tainment, costlier and more artificial, London now, like Madrid and Paris, found itself with the choice of two. In 1661 Sir William Davenant's Duke's Company opened the Lincoln's Inn Fields Theatre, which was replaced in 1671 by the more splendid Dorset Garden Theatre (built by Wren) for a successful decade; and in 1663 the King's Company, managed by Thomas Killigrew, opened the Theatre Royal in Bridges Street and in 1674 transferred to the newly built Drury Lane Theatre, also by Wren.

It was the Lincoln's Inn Fields Theatre that registered the changes in attitude and approach most clearly. It was the first stage in England to employ scenery in the Continental manner and the first to boast a proscenium arch. From the point of view of English theatrical traditions and their assimilation of some of the thinking underlying the baroque conception of theatricality, this was an innovation marking a major departure, since it appeared to demonstrate the clear separation of stage and audience and their separate worlds: the play now opened up like an animated picture, the actors' voices alone reaching beyond the frame as they declaimed their heroic couplets. Yet was this what was happening? And was this the real intention behind this technical innovation or, rather, was this belated adoption of features already being developed elsewhere? Curiously enough, the development of this particular feature had very different results elsewhere. In Vienna the marriage of the Emperor Leopold I (1640-1705) to the Infanta

Margarita Teresa (1666), which had prompted the composition of
Lohenstein's play *Sophonisbe*, also occasioned the construction of
the magnificent theatre Auf der Cortina, partly in order to
demonstrate Vienna's superiority over the Paris of Louis XIV.
Destroyed during the Turkish siege of 1683, it was probably the
supreme example in all Europe of the baroque stage, thanks largely
to the inventiveness of its designer Ludovico Ottavio Burnacini
(1636-1707), brilliant exponent of the cosmopolitan art of
cunningly fusing heterogeneous stylistic elements into a stunningly
yet meaningfully impressive whole. The proscenium arch he
designed for the emperor's great theatre in Vienna must have had
the opposite effect to that ascribed to its modest London counterparts, or so one gathers; instead of separating stage from audience,
it actually served to bring them together by suggesting that the
stage was in fact an extra dimension of the audience's reality, and
linked as closely to it as are dreams to life. But for illusion to
become one with reality, for the world of the stage, of sets and
scenery, dance and declamation, to extend and enhance the
everyday world requires artistic and financial resources such as
seventeenth-century England was seldom, if ever, prepared to
expend. Elsewhere things were different: in Madrid, Vienna and
Paris the visual realization of the age's ethos amply justified the
spending of untold resources, and the same holds true of Rome's
entertainments and the seven or more opera houses of Venice too.

The most lavish stage entertainment ever mounted in
seventeenth-century Europe was the one which inaugurated
Vienna's vast and majestic new theatre, Auf der Cortina. It took
place in July 1668, and was devised by Burnacini to celebrate the
birthday of the new Empress. *Il Pomo d'Oro* was the opera
produced for the occasion, and it was itself the culmination of the
brilliant career of its composer, Pietro Cesti (1623-69), a musician
of ebullient artistic personality and dubious morals, who was widely
renowned for the richness and fertility of his musical invention and
had come to rival, even to outshine, Cavalli himself. Cesti, who
adopted the name Antonio on becoming a Franciscan friar, had
captured the spectacle-loving musical public of Venice in the late
1640s, and continued to delight them until in 1666 he was
summoned to Vienna to take up the office of deputy master of the
emperor's music. He had even been contemplated as a possible
alternative to Cavalli in the complicated case of the commission of

an Italian opera to celebrate the marriage of Louis XIV: now, in 1668, one year before his death by poison, his creative genius co-incided with the destinies of European states and produced a major cultural event. The great moment of his life had come, its brilliance captured for us, if only faintly, by the Burnacini stage designs that have survived and by the music he wrote, but which we seldom if ever hear. Yet what an extraordinary achievement this was, this produc-tion of *Il Pomo d'Oro*, when designer, composer, musicians, per-formers — a staff of hundreds spending many thousands — fleet-ingly evoked a whole incredible world of myth with the sole aim of giving pleasure to the few for a few hours. Admittedly the empress may have smiled, and the emperor have taken pride in the thought that Austria had stolen a march on France and Spain. Yet the transience of the whole project is its dominant, its lasting quality, a transience which almost seems to justify the enormous expense, so supremely did it epitomize the values of the age.

The opera opened with a 'programme overture' — the first in musical history — which painted the scene and anticipated the action, and then the curtain rose and Burnacini's theatre came gloriously into its own as all four elements and all the gods and demigods of ancient myth sprang to life in sound and colour across the proscenium arch and before the audience's gaze. Dark Hades, kingdom of the dead, with Proserpine, the exiled queen, lamenting in tones of anguish her life deprived of light; and then we are transported to bright Olympus, where feasting gods regale them-selves among the floating clouds, until Discord throws the apple in, and thus involves the fate of all mankind. The Judgement of Paris follows, and that choice the baroque age could understand so fully: empire over Asia and Europe, Juno's offer; mastery over men in battle, that of Minerva; and the lovely Helen, embodiment of beauty, an irresistible reward which wins the golden apple for Venus. Yet once Paris has chosen and set off in amorous pursuit of Spartan Helen, the Trojan War has started and the bloodshed and the struggle for supremacy begin. The mouth of Hell gapes open: what a stage set! Paris, caught in a storm at sea, implores the aid of Venus, and the stage becomes a watery vision in which nereids and tritons come swimming to his assistance, then turns into a field of battle on which scores of extras engage in displays of valour — not to mention real horses, and elephants too. Thus Mars and Venus triumph, and are seen to: love, war and the omnipresent sea from

which the goddess rose and which can never extinguish the fires of
passion; opportunities, all of them, for displays of fustian pomp
that are also daring feats of the creative visual imagination. Until
finally Jove, tiring of strife, commands his eagle to swoop down —
the heraldic touch was pleasing — and snatch the golden apple so
that in a gesture of appropriate finality the symbolic fruit can be
taken from the contesting goddesses and awarded by the god to
Austria's new Spanish empress who in her person unites the
qualities and virtues of all three, for only she is as wise as she is
powerful, and as lovely as she is wise.

The mythological subject was an old one, and had often been
treated during the Renaissance, for, with its perennial theme of a
young man's choice, it had long exerted a considerable ethical
appeal. But the way it was handled here, like the motives
underlying the performance and the scenic features that made it
memorable, clearly brings out the values of the baroque and
illustrates its objectives. The cosmopolitan collaboration of
composer and designer, musicians, singers, stagehands and decorators, mechanics and menials demonstrates how very much the
baroque was a style, a culture and even an ethos which did not so
much destroy the boundaries of nationality as actually transcend
them. The only boundaries it recognized were those between this
world and the next and between our reality and the realm of
dreams, and even these it was intent on crossing. And then the
venue too, Vienna, was so apt. Capital of the Holy Roman Empire
(of a Germany, that is, which included much that was by no means
German), it also felt it was the centre of a universal empire. Since
its ruling house, the Habsburgs, also ruled Spain and the Spanish
dominions overseas — Africa, the Americas and the Far East — the
Habsburg possessions had become known as the 'empire over which
the sun never set', an empire which had reached out beyond the
Pillars of Hercules, the traditional limit of the ancient world, to
embrace the entire globe and thus bear tangible political and
commercial witness to its spherical shape. It was a situation that lent
itself to allegorical representation. Vienna was used to thinking on
an imperial scale, and not surprisingly it did so now in 1668, in
celebration of the wife of the Emperor Leopold, and herself the
daughter of his Spanish brother-in-law and uncle — a marriage
which exemplified the traditional Habsburg policy of controlling
discord and gaining strength through holy matrimony to the greater
glory of the family, the state and the Catholic religion.

This mythological entertainment with machines, music and mime was close enough in spirit to the kind of festive allegory presented in the 'colosseum' at Buen Retiro for the new empress to have felt quite at home in it. After all, persons of her rank, background and upbringing shared a modicum at least of classical knowledge and political awareness, and quite enough to appreciate the allegorical argument and pick up its topical allusions. And what she watched in Vienna, if not in Spanish, was at least in Italian, by now the *lingua franca* of the baroque age and, ever since, of music. For Viennese imperial entertainments preferred to shun German, despite the impressive achievements of which it had shown itself capable in the hands of talented and imaginative writers such as Lohenstein. But German was too provincial for this centre of universal empire, and too unlikely to satisfy the taste of a court and aristocracy drawn as much from Bohemia and northern Italy as from the many principalities and states of Germany itself. Italian provided the sounds of cosmopolitan culture with a Roman patina, and this was a quality which made it very widely acceptable.

The theatrical delights of *Il Pomo d'Oro* are ones which have vanished almost beyond recall. Something perhaps of its exuberance and significance can be sensed by an imagination that has assimilated examples of baroque painting — nereids, tritons, battles, gods, goddesses, and those imaginary landscapes of Arcadian calm or rugged terror which artists such as Cesti's admirer Salvator Rosa could evoke — and heard samples of the heroic declamation and poignant lament, the dignified choruses and orchestral colours associated with Italian seventeenth-century opera. But, even if the eye and ear are to some extent able to recapture the distant strains and faded colours of Cesti's music and Burnacini's sets, much remains elusive. *Il Pomo d'Oro*, like all its innumerable but less famous counterparts, was after all a highly composite work of art which exploited the distinctive resources not only of music and décor but of actors and dancers and of stage machinery, too, which animated the living painting into movement in time to the rhythms of the music and in harmony with the emotions it expressed. Indeed this attention to movement, which was such an integral part of these stage productions, was perhaps their most quintessentially baroque quality, since the baroque is nothing if not a rejection of classical calm and of those static ideals which characterize the age that preceded it and the age that was to follow. The spectators, used to motionless painting which sought to

capture movement in an eternal present, delighted to behold
clouds float, waves billow and chariots descend from heaven, while
abysmal chasms yawned: the painting comes to life in movement
and sound within the transient dimension of time, the living world
re-created on a stage by the genius and artifice of man.

The great achievements of the seventeenth-century stage —
operas like those of Monteverdi and Cavalli, Cesti and Lully, plays
like those of Lohenstein, Pierre Corneille, Calderón and Vondel —
were achievements which transcended the frontiers of nations in
their emotional and intellectual appeal, in their aesthetic assumptions or, when their actual language did create a barrier, at least in
the universal familiarity and relevance of their themes and subject
matter. But, more than that, they also repaid the age's debt to the
traditional image of the world as a stage by making of the theatrical
stage a world — a world which was characterized by even greater
transitoriness than the real one, but which in the brief compass of a
few hours' performance allowed resourceful, creative minds to
conjure up splendours that seemed to contemporaries to outshine
by far the realities of the everyday world — no mean achievement
considering the surroundings in which such performances took
place, splendid palaces or cities famous for their wealth and beauty.
And so convinced were contemporaries of the reality of illusion in
the world they lived in and the lives they led that they were ready
both to appreciate and to create by every means and technique at
their disposal the illusion of reality. Generally speaking, the
baroque imagination delighted above all in the creation of an
illusory reality more opulent and splendid than any the ordinary
world could offer, and chose audaciously to presume that man
could use his wealth and artistry to outshine his maker.

Yet it was from this same basic urge so characteristic of the period
that the impetus came, in France especially, to create the illusion of
a reality less extravagant and fanciful by rigorously observing the
notorious three unities of time, place and action supposed to stem
from Aristotle and the art of ancient Greece. 'For the stage being
the representation of the world, and the actions in it, how can it be
imagined that the picture of human life can be more exact than life
itself is?' asked Dryden in the Dedication to his *The Rival Ladies* in
1664. But it was a notion which had no more justification for it
than that of the Italians that their opera was a genuine resuscitation
of the tragedy of ancient Greece. Both schools of thought required

this kind of justification for their innovatory creative views, for their age was marked by the belief that what the ancients had said and done carried the whole force of truth. The quarrel between the Ancients and the Moderns had not yet begun: this was still a time of cultural coexistence in which that old saw *antiquissimum quodque verissimum* was axiomatic and self-evident, yet in no sense a straitjacket hampering imaginative experimentation. In the light of it both the 'verisimilitude' of French classical tragedy and the extraordinary phantasmagoria of Venetian opera were explicable, for both were intent on opening up an alternative dimension of reality. Nor were these two theatrical phenomena as diametrically opposed as many critics then and since have thought, for it proved quite possible for the genius of Louis XIV's favourite court musician, the Italian Jean-Baptiste Lully (1632-87), who had first attracted wider attention with his ballets for Cavalli's *Ercole amante*, to reconcile them in the series of lyric tragedies, as he called them, which he opened with his *Cadmus et Hermione* in 1673. These fused many of the qualities of Racine's tragic re-creations of the classical heritage from *Andromaque* on (1667) with the visual and aural delights of baroque opera. Truth and fancy, sincerity and artifice, the tragic world torn between passion and reason and the operatic world of opulent melody and stately recitative: the combination was not an easy one and not even Lully achieved it overnight. From the wider European point of view it was also one of the outstanding cultural achievements of the age, and as such did a great deal to establish France's deserved position of cultural as well as political hegemony as the great years of the baroque in Europe drew to a close.

Behind the grandiose façade what was there? As diversion succeeded diversion in an endless succession of routs and ridottos, comedies and ballets, hunts and carousels, masques and masquerades, until it seemed that life itself was one prolonged festivity, what were the realities? What did the thinking courtier think? 'Las cosas no pasan por lo que son, sino por lo que parecen' — 'Things do not pass for what they are but for what they seem; and many are satisfied with appearances', the Spanish Jesuit Gracián observed in 1647. 'It is not enough to be in the right if the outward appearance of your action is not.' To the clearsighted, sincere philosopher façades and festivities may indeed be illusions since they do not correspond to reality; but to the average honest man of the world, steering his way across the stage of life and acting his part in the game of living to his best ability, the need to assume appearances and indulge in illusions was just as essential as it was for a monarch strutting about the theatre of European diplomacy and warmongering, and indulging in displays of mythological pomp and martial grandeur in a very real socio-political world. Life is a constant struggle for self-preservation against the malice and hostility of one's fellows, and self-assertion is the obvious way to achieve a position of supremacy in others' eyes and to maintain it. What every man and woman of some position in society and wise to the ways of the world was constantly and every day doing was exactly what in heightened form the baroque stage was presenting for its audiences' pleasure and admiration. For, like the heroes of the stage, each member of the audience was striving to use his native wit and ingenuity to impress his fellows and project himself upon them while at the same time appearing to accommodate himself to the requirements of society. To be successfully yourself without offending the conventions of society was as dangerous and required as much skill as it took to create an original work of art without offending against the rules of aesthetic tradition or the taste of society. No wonder some of the most notable exponents of the practical art of survival and self-enhancement in the seventeenth century also took particular interest and delight in promoting the creation and production of works that mirrored their ever-present reality in perhaps loftier and more glamorous terms.

Cardinal Richelieu and his successor Mazarin, like the great monarch whom they served and for whom they prepared the way, represent in a French context what was a general phenomenon. If Cardinal Mazarin's primary motive in staging an Italian opera to mark Louis XIV's Spanish marriage was, as he put it, to dazzle Europe, this does not for a moment mean that he, Louis, France and indeed Europe did not respond to the enterprise with extraordinary interest and delight: after all, a fine exterior is the best witness to inward perfection; and wealth, power and taste must be displayed with emphasis if they are to be generally perceived and appreciated. In other words, the glory attached to such events, and which seemed to justify the squandering of untold resources on them, was a highly prized commodity which, by and large, was shared out to the satisfaction of all concerned — nation, monarch, musicians, designers, performers, and society in the shape of an audience, too. And, underlying the age's ready admiration for such displays, as well as its fondness for the image of the world as a stage, there was a fundamental belief in the practical value of culture itself, both as a symbolic expression of status and as a fundamental factor of civilization; for men are but barbarians by birth, and culture alone saves them from their natural barbarity. Assumed or genuine, the role of art-lover was therefore one which most men of the world found themselves playing in baroque Europe. In moments of tribulation or of spiritual insight they might derive some consolation from the realization, equally characteristic of the period, that all our roles are only played on the stage of life. In the tiring-room of Death we all become mere actors again: the distinctions between us, which had seemed to matter so much, were only ones of costume.

Over the entrance to the Globe Theatre in London had been written the Latin words 'Totus mundus agit histrionem' (the whole world plays the actor). The inscription probably derived from a medieval English source, *Policraticus*, by John of Salisbury, a philosophical work dedicated to Thomas à Becket and significantly reprinted at strategic moments throughout the period — 1595, 1622, 1639, 1664, 1677 — dates corresponding, all of them, with periods of pronounced theatrical activity in Europe. But the medieval English churchman admits that the notion of the world as a stage which embellishes his account of the diversions enjoyed by courtiers is formulated after Petronius, the Roman courtier who wrote the notorious *Satyricon* and acted as the arbiter of fashion at the court of the Emperor Nero, whose victim he, like Seneca, finally became. Not much has survived of Petronius' witty and licentious novel in the Hellenistic manner, but enough to conjure up a world which seventeenth-century courtiers and men of wit and fashion felt had much in common with their own. They too lived in a climate that favoured ostentatious displays of wealth and pomp; they too set off in pursuit of pleasure while sensing the futility of their quest and the vanity of all such cravings. Seldom if ever since the Rome of the tyrant Nero had such importance been attached to outward show, and to the enhancement and setting of things: banquets and outdoor collations, tournaments and chases, operas and ballets required settings as did melodies and portraits, and indeed the human being himself — and in each and every case the setting was of paramount importance to the baroque mentality.

Nero showing off his horsemanship to the Roman mob or appearing on stage in musical spectacles to the applause of his courtiers, and earning for his imperial voice and person the epithets of deities; exploring by night and in disguise the underworld of Rome, or building his sumptuous golden palace and surrounding it with parks and woodlands; writing high-flown poetry, collecting paintings and sculptures, likened by sycophantic contemporaries to Hercules, Apollo and the Emperor Augustus: there is indeed a remarkable similarity between the Roman portrayed by Tacitus and Suetonius and the monarchs and lesser mortals of the baroque age. Yet it would be quite wrong to think that they were simply intent on imitating antiquity. Such imitations are for many reasons — historical, economic, sociological — an impossibility. Rather, to them, the past's anticipation of their own present was valuable evidence of continuity, and proved to them the unchanging truth and validity of their view of human life. The real Nero, persecutor of Seneca and Petronius, of St Peter and St Paul, the art-loving tyrant who had once raved and ranted on the Roman stage, now joined those other protagonists of drama — Hercules, Paris, Oedipus, and the others — that was all. And baroque spectators, like their counterparts in ancient Rome, knew that once the performance of the play was over, its text, as Petronius had said, might well survive in a book, but the actors' real faces would be restored to them once the make-up was removed.

2

Masks & masques

'This masquerading is a most glorious invention.... For to go
unknown is the next degree to going invisible,' observes Rodophil
in Dryden's *Marriage à la Mode* (1672), a richly rewarding blend of
worldly elegance and pastoral convention. Yet his is surely a case of
the fictitious character repeating what must have been said by
countless people in all the languages of cultured Europe during an
age which accorded disguise and dressing-up an importance not
enjoyed before or since. Was it flippancy or deadly earnest? Or,
rather, the token of that middle area where truth is uncertain and
the unknown opens up its beguiling or disturbing perspectives?
Certainly the increasing importance given to masque and masquerade as society's favourite diversions coincided from the later
sixteenth century onwards with a growing delight in going, as
Rodophil says, 'unknown', and in discovering as you do so the
truth about your fellow men through deliberate concealment of
your own identity. But the game is only feasible and socially
acceptable if played by all, and an awareness of this essential
condition can alone save the delightful masquerade from dissolving
into appalling pandemonium. In comedy the removal of the mask
will invariably indicate that the conventional happy ending is in
sight. But if the comedy were not a comedy, that is, a conventional
theatrical entertainment, destined for a preordained dénouement,
the danger would always be present that the mask's removal might
reveal the hideous grinning face of Death. In other words the

distance, at once long and very, very short between the sequined vizard glimpsed at playhouse or court festivity and the mask as thin and fragile screen between ignorant illusion and revelation of the starkest truth, represents one of the fundamental dimensions of baroque culture, and links together areas which may at first seem very far apart. In fact they are intimately related, and common to the manners, the thinking and the art of baroque Europe.

Whence this infatuation with concealment and disguise? To trace its principal sources is in a sense to define some of the many complex factors that went into the making of the baroque mentality and which are reflected in its art. On one level it was, no doubt, the stiffness and forced unnaturalness of court life and courtly behaviour that led many people to seek relief in the delights offered by disguise: there are similarities here to the relaxation many aristocratic people found in pastoral play and poetry. But why could court life not be less staid, less formal? It is a question which at once occurs to us; but to the European of the sixteenth and seventeenth centuries there was no reason for asking it. To him, court was a reality; indeed, it was the centre of social reality, the arbiter of taste and fashion, and the obvious place wherein to seek preferment and make a career. The whole drift of European political and social history from the late Middle Ages onwards was towards the centralizing glorification of authority and government, and of their embodiment, the prince. For was not the crown the chief ornament of the body politic? The court, a radiance emanating from it like rays from the sun or avenues from a palace? Yet power is shifting, its supports treacherous: of that the age was equally aware. The essential instability of all secular human institutions had therefore to be shored up by all the weight of time-honoured tradition and sacrosanct convention. In many ways the courts of the 'age of absolutism', both secular and religious, were truer heirs of that Constantinople which fell to the Turk in 1453 than the humanist culture of Renaissance Italy, for the royal households of baroque sovereigns evolved a truly Byzantine mystique around their absolute yet socially and religiously circumscribed masters. Hierarchy, ceremonial and stifling convention ruled the day; only in disguise and masquerade could the rigid forms of courtly decorum — the bonds of golden slavery — be momentarily forgotten; for it is a characteristic feature of this loose and amorphous type of court entertainment to culminate in a direct or implicit eulogy of its most important participant.

Though this may account in large measure for the popularity of masques and masquerades at the courts of seventeenth-century Europe, it would be mistaken to overlook deeper and perhaps more elemental sources. For here too, as in its theatrical or pastoral propensities, the baroque age was drawing on deep and long-standing cultural traditions. Masque and masquerade were particularly prominent during two specific seasons of the year: Twelfth Night, especially in England, and Carnival, the period leading from the Christmas festivities to a culminating point on Shrove Tuesday, the eve of Lent, in all those countries which took a traditionally Roman Catholic view of the spiritual year and of Lenten fasting. Now winter solstice, Saturnalia and spring's awakening have for centuries been associated with forms of revelry and merrymaking combining half-understood symbolism with invitations to lighthearted relaxation. And on these ancient traditions the baroque age drew deeply. In the first place it was itself so instinctively aware of the half-hidden allegories implicit in all things. Then, too, like the later Middle Ages, which had brought Shrovetide festivities and customs to a high flowering, it was a period obsessed with the ceaseless rotation of fortune's wheel and which had not entirely forgotten the irresistible dance in which masked Death will pick his partners. It is therefore true to say that just as it produced a revival of certain aspects of Byzantine civilization, like court ritual and endlessly long-drawn-out 'Greek' romances, so too it witnessed a largely unwitting development of late medieval popular traditions, often transformed in outward appearance, of course, and varying from place to place, and which were to be seen at their most lavish and profligate in that most prosperous and Byzantine of European cities, Venice. A third factor, however, had arisen which did very much to distinguish the baroque approach from that of the late Middle Ages. One of the main legacies it received from the Renaissance which preceded it was its knowledgeable awareness of classical antiquity and the precedents it offered. The realization that ancient Greece and Rome had associated masks with tragedy and comedy provided a reassuring precedent of just this kind. The baroque age appreciated this deeply. Yet it was an age of contradictions, and curiously enough it failed to make the wearing of masks obligatory on the serious stage, but chose instead to transfer the habit to the audience. In the baroque theatres of Venice, for instance, or

London, the real world (and especially the fair sex) watched, masked and invisible, as the counterfeit world on stage visibly mirrored its reality and finally unmasked it to reveal what lay behind. Such meaningful make-believe is of its essence.

If the donning of a mask or vizard provided a substitute for invisibility and allowed distinctions of rank, and the behaviour they entailed, to be forgotten in a search for wider, richer, less foreseeable experience, the cult of the masque as an art form in Jacobean and Caroline England, and the development of similar fashions in other European countries, indicated a compulsive longing for a wider aesthetic experience which would at one and the same time dazzle the eye, beguile the ear, entertain the mind and involve the body too. Décor, costume, music, poetry and dance were all exploited in order to devise entertainments the like of which had never been seen before, and whose sumptuous fusion of so many arts was actually enhanced by the certain knowledge that they would leave nothing behind them but a memory in people's minds or a myth retold to astonish future generations. Never has so much ingenuity, such flair and artistic talent, gone into the designing and production of entertainments of such meteoric transience as these baroque masques and masquerades. Whole fortunes were spent on them. Palaces and gardens were transformed by staffs of hundreds to provide their settings; costumes, decorations and machines were devised with no care for cost and no eye whatever on future fame. For this was the apotheosis of the fugitive moment, the supreme aesthetic admission that time is fleeting, that nothing is permanent, and that a moment is enough to reveal and swallow all. In the age's many grandiose firework displays this was literally the case. The sable vault of night would be transformed by human wit and ingenuity into a brightness that exceeded day; and as genial pyrotechnical skill engineered some triumphant emblem or device to appear in fiery letters before an astonished multitude, it seemed as though the brightest of the natural elements had been momentarily enslaved by man. For was this not the age which actually used real gold to imitate the licking flame?

Though Louis XIV's Versailles was in many respects destined to become the setting of a poised and classical culture very unlike the baroque, its marbled, gilded and mirrored halls and, above all, its vast and versatile gardens were the scene of some of the most spectacular of these seventeenth-century diversions. The wealth of

France, the extrovert personality of its sovereign and the gathering together there of one of Europe's most illustrious aristocracies assured Versailles of a magnificence which even Vienna and Madrid could hardly equal, let alone any of the courts and country residences that dotted the landscape of Germany and England. Yet the extent to which the French monarch's taste and lifestyle were shaped and conditioned by Spanish and Italian influences is not always realized: his forceful mother, Anne of Austria, was the daughter of a Spanish Habsburg king, as was his unprepossessing wife, while his grandmother, Marie de' Medici, was the Florentine princess whose arrival in France as queen to the ex-Protestant Henry IV was immortalized in a series of florid apotheoses painted by Rubens in the 1620s. Nevertheless it is equally true and perhaps also more symptomatic of France's subsequent cultural development that the greatest Italian baroque genius in the field of the applied arts, Bernini, should have met with a rebuff in Paris when at the height of his powers and despite the hitherto favourable climate there and his own richly deserved reputation. A competition held in 1665 for designs to complete the Louvre palace was finally won not by the Italian, as had first seemed likely, but by the French classicizing architects Perrault, Le Vau and Le Brun: the way was open for the gradual transformation of Louis's intimately baroque Versailles into the vast and stately edifice which was to reflect a new image of monarchy and set the fashion for the age to come.

From the architectural point of view the defeat of Bernini's high baroque in France was of momentous importance. The experience of Italian baroque artists in other domains was rather similar. In spectacular entertainment, choreography, music and song, Italians had come to play a dominant part especially during the administration of their compatriot Cardinal Mazarin during the 1650s, and in 1660 the most successful and respected Italian operatic composer of the day, Pier Francesco Cavalli, was commissioned by the cardinal to compose an opera to mark the satisfactory negotiation of the Peace of the Pyrenees between France and Spain, and to celebrate the young French king's marriage to his cousin, the Infanta Maria Teresa. The elderly musician was invited to leave Venice, scene of his many triumphs, and come to Paris to supervise the sumptuous production of his appropriately entitled *Ercole amante*, or 'Hercules in Love'. This was due to take place in a vast

new auditorium being built in the Tuileries Palace for a capacity of
over 5000 by the distinguished Italian designer Gaspare Vigarani,
who had recently succeeded to the position held by his even more
original compatriot Giacomo Torelli, nicknamed the 'great wizard'
(*il gran stregone*). Never had Italian influence been more blatantly
in evidence in France. But the cardinal's death the next year, and
the king's prompt assumption of personal and absolute power,
marked a turning point as important for the development of the
baroque as the accesssion of the Emperor Leopold I in 1658 or the
1660 Restoration in England. When the theatre was finally ready in
1662, the long-deferred six-hour performance of *Ercole amante* at
last took place; but what stole all the fire were the ballets added by
the king's favourite musician Lully. For the king was the cynosure
of all, and a fine dancer who on this occasion exhausted his partner
by his extrovert performance in what amounted to a court masque.
Meanwhile the rumbling din of Vigarani's gigantic stage machines,
capable some of them of raising and lowering up to 200 people on
painted golden clouds, and the hubbub of the huge audience
enraptured at the sight, drowned the soft harmonies and melting
voices of Cavalli's Venetian music.

Vigarani's dream had been the realization of an infinite perspective by artificial means, a theatrical counterpart to the ceilings and
altarpieces of churches painted to seem open to the skies; the
theatre he produced turned out to be a shortlived white elephant, far
too big and unwieldy for an age which adored exaggeration and
grandeur but lacked the technological means to amplify vision and
sound. For the composer, too, the future in France held out no
prospects; disappointed, he made his slow way back to Venice.
France had no use for his affecting blend of limpid lyricism and
comic verve. Its self-confident and splendour-loving young
monarch was assuming a new and different role and entering on a
more formal phase of the baroque, leading much of Europe behind
him.

The 1660s were, however, to see the successful production of a
number of French stage entertainments which retained many of the
features associated with the Venetian love of disguise and intrigue,
unfolding in a colourful sequence of slumbers, dreams, prophecies
and farewells — a blend of serious and comic elements which
Restoration London was in turn to imitate in stage entertainments
such as Purcell's *King Arthur* (1691) and *The Fairy Queen* (1692),

or the reworking Dryden in 1690 offered London of Molière's comedy *Amphitryon*, first played with great success in Paris in 1668.

'Amphitryon' is perhaps the most characteristic of baroque subjects. Molière (1622-73) modelled his elegantly entertaining version of it on a Roman comedy by Plautus, again demonstrating the age's delight in its classical precedents, but not without some awareness of the same subject's earlier French treatment by one of Europe's major baroque dramatists, Jean de Rotrou, in 1637. In Molière's comedy hidden identity, divine prophecy, amorous inter- play, mythological allusion and contemporary relevance all combine in order to account for the legendary conception of the future demigod and lover, Hercules, begotten of the beautiful and virtuous Alcmene by Jove himself in the guise of her adored husband, the Greek general Amphitryon. The audience, so the story goes, smiled to detect allusions in this risqué subject to their king's affair with Madame de Montespan; a high-born lady's tragicomic inability to distinguish between lover and husband, god and man, was calculated to amuse spectators as sophisticated and experienced in the ways of the world as those at the court of France. And Molière had genius and taste enough to ensure that the begetter's divinity flattered his most Christian king without arousing the disapproval of the Church. Perils navigated with such dramatic knowhow and poetic ease only enhanced the baroque qualities of a comic masterpiece very far removed from the poise and balance of his more classical comedies, and which is delicious evidence of the fact that Molière, as well as being the inventor of the later European comedy of character and manners, was also a brilliant exponent of the earlier tradition, with its delight in parallels and contrasts, almost irreconcilable paradoxes, extra- ordinary situations and theatrical surprises.

It is said that what delighted the first audiences of the play was the use made of stage machinery in the Prologue, when Mercury, messenger of the gods, by Jove's command arrests the chariot of the goddess Night so as to prolong his divine master's amorous embraces, and also in the final scene, when at last the supreme deity radiantly descends from heaven in his true guise to enlighten the mystified and desperate mortal, Amphitryon: 'There's nothing dishonourable in sharing with a god, and is it not glorious to be the rival of one? For Jove, embellished with all his eternal glory, failed to triumph over the virtue of Alcmène: what her ardent heart so readily bestowed was given to her husband, not her god.' Thus the decorum of divinity is restored. Sosie, Amphitryon's servant, wryly comments: 'Lord Jupiter knows how to gild the pill; but it might be best to say no more about what actually took place.' The blend of impudent irony and self-assured dignity is extraordinary — or, rather, the avoidance of all offence to honour, rank or good taste, without the least sacrifice of verve, wit or erotic innuendo. But underlying Molière's courtly extravaganza on updated mythology and Olympian gallantry there is another dimension of the play which is even more fundamentally baroque. And this is the crisis of identity articulated by the comic sequence of identities concealed and revealed. In Mercury's opening dialogue with the goddess Night, Jove's need to conceal his divine identity is revealed as a desire to savour all degrees and conditions, and thereby to escape from the misery of life-imprisonment in his glorious and majestic role. A god makes himself man in this play not so as to redeem mankind but in order to escape from the decorum demanded by mankind of its divinities, and to relax for a moment in the arms of his most perfect creature. But Jove is too conscious of the fact of his absolute divinity to be able to forget his identity for long. His pleasures granted and his desires gratified, he reverts to the pomp and authority of his proper station. Sosie, the servant, is not allowed to forget his condition either. His substitution by his divine double, Mercury, is introduced by a repartee which points directly to the baroque theme pervading the entire play:

Mercury	Qui va là?
Sosie	Moi.
Mercury	Qui, moi?

And that theme is brilliantly realized in dramatic terms when, towards the end, the outraged Amphitryon desperately draws his sword to fight his other self in single combat, and has to be held back by his associates from committing what, wittily yet almost tragically, amounts to suicide. Of course the king of the gods saves the day, unmasks himself, and in an impressive display of grandeur and magnanimity dispels the illusion to reveal the reality that underlay appearances. After all, the play is a comedy; but, being by Molière, it cannot help suggesting deeper implications.

The complex interplay of comedy and tragedy implicit in the

baroque fondness for concealed motive and assumed mask was given its most penetrating treatment in one of the seventeenth century's most famous comic dramas, *Tartuffe* (1664, revised version 1667, final version 1669). By the time he came to produce *Amphitryon*, Molière had learnt from the bitter experience of this earlier play, subtitled 'The Impostor', to trim his comic insights and to be more circumspect about overstepping the remarkably generous moral and religious limits of the baroque stage. *Tartuffe* incurred the hostility of the Company of the Holy Sacrament, a highly honourable secret society devoted to good works and the cause of Catholic reform. 'Do not annoy the pious, they will never forgive you,' the king advised his greatest playwright; but Molière could not resist the creative urge to write what was soon to be regarded as the most effective of all comic exposures of self-seeking duplicity masquerading as sanctimonious self-righteousness. Orgon, a gentleman of average means and judgement, is hood-winked by the hypocrite he has taken in, and remains obdurately deaf to his brother-in-law's Act I denunciation of the impostor in the form of an analysis of what may well be a universal human situation, but which is defined here in a sequence of characteristic-ally baroque images, that of the mask and face being the most striking precisely because of its links both with theatrical traditions and with seventeenth-century social behaviour:

> Hé quoi! vous ne ferez nulle distinction
> Entre l'hypocrisie et la dévotion?
> Voulez-vous les traiter d'un semblable langage,
> Et rendre même honneur au masque qu'au visage;
> Égaler l'artifice à la sincérité,
> Confondre l'apparence avec la vérité,
> Estimer le fantôme autant que la personne,
> Et la fausse monnaie à l'égal de la bonne?

Nowhere, in fact, does one come across a more succinct catalogue of basic baroque themes than in Cléante's speech in the first act of this long-established masterpiece of the French classical stage. Hypocrisy and religious fervour; levels of language and diction; the relative honour due to mask and face; the widespread tendency to equate sincerity and affectation; the mistaking of appearances for truth and of spectres for real people, false alloy for sterling, gilt for gold: these are all of them fundamental to the baroque and therefore fundamental too for any assessment and understanding of its artistic and cultural manifestations. The fact that so very many of these manifestations were the product of piety, proselytizing zeal and mystical devotion brings home something of the unique irony of Molière's dramatization of villainy disguised as holiness. Here comic unmasking is a deeply apposite form of entertainment.

Where make-believe was an integral and everyday part of social behaviour, it was actually possible to explore the most unlikely confusions of appearance and reality without even having recourse to the traditional masks of Italian comedy. All over Europe audiences were always ready to suspend their judgement and allow themselves the pleasure of being seduced into worlds of fantastic adventure and romance. Appearances were exulted in for their own sake by men and women less heedful of the underlying truth than their preachers, confessors or teachers might have wished. Stark spiritual and social realities are never easy to stomach. In Restoration England playgoers were notoriously addicted to extravagant displays of heroics which, at first sight, had little to do with contemporary life but had much in common with the artistic mood of Europe as a whole. In Venice, Rome, Naples and the other major cities of Italy opera-goers had long demanded distraction and variety, grandiloquence and colour. But the most striking instance of extravagant popular entertainment actually fusing with an audaciously novel exploration of the whole question of personal identity actually occurred in France, with the play which was quick to prove the greatest theatrical success of the seventeenth century: *Timocrate* (1657) by Pierre Corneille's younger brother, Thomas. *Timocrate* enjoyed the rare privilege of being put on, it is said, in both Paris theatres simultaneously. Soon the most sophisticated audience in Europe had taken it to their hearts. In the late 1650s, not to have seen Thomas Corneille's extravagant tragedy was not to have lived; yet any student of French classical literature will know that the play simply does not figure in the accepted poetic canon. Why? Because it was bad? No: but because it represents one of the climaxes of baroque stage entertainment in Europe, and can only be enjoyed if seen in terms of meaningful make-believe. As an aesthetic experience *Timocrate* dazzles with its verve and versatility. Easy on ear and eye, it remains a difficult work just to read, precisely because it is such a *tour de force* of high-flown equivocation and dramatic suspense.

At the centre of the intrigue is Timocrate himself, the warrior-king of Crete, who, as the play opens, is attacking Argos, a Greek state whose military weakness has been largely offset of late by the efforts of a valiant young hero called Cléomène. Both, being gallant men, are suitors for the hand of Ériphile, the beautiful princess of Argos. Feats of extraordinary valour and protestations of undying love lead swiftly on to the foreseeable: Timocrate is taken captive by Cléomène. The verdict is spoken: the one shall die, the other win the hand of the princess. But now comes that astonishing baroque *coup de théâtre* which so delighted contemporary audiences, and which takes the central theme one further. Cléomène reveals that he is none other than — Timocrate. 'Timocrate haï dans Cléomène aimé', one loved, the other hated: one the ardent lover, the other a foreign king intent on a political marriage. Unlike Alcmène in Molière's comedy, the heroine of this heroic tragedy can easily distinguish between the two: yet in this case they are one and the same! There is only one solution to the dilemma, the union of both realms so as to make the best of both worlds. Thus noble acceptance of an unlikely situation forms the only acceptable dénouement of a play determined to entertain rather than to harrow, and in which, as in *Amphitryon*, the French public could, if it wanted, see the reflected image of its admired and amorous king, or simply enjoy the panache of the courtly life he represented, and that elegance of style and sentiment which was its official ideal. A less than perfect social and political reality superficially decked out with the borrowed plumes of heroism and romance? Or heroism and romance transfigured into a pleasing confection of gallant sentiments and hollow gestures? Something of both, no doubt, but certainly also an enchantingly high-spirited exploration of a very serious baroque preoccupation: the problem of identity, and with it the whole question of appearance and reality.

To twentieth-century German cultural historians especially, the problem of appearance and reality seems fundamental to the culture of the baroque age in Europe and the real key to the whole baroque phenomenon. *Schein und Sein*, they call it, and the rhyme lends added force and conviction to the phrase. Now certainly the German writers of the age were particularly adept at graphic depictions of the juxtaposition of *Schein* and *Sein*, and sometimes capable of creations more penetrating and introspective than the English court masque, the Venetian opera, or the *ballet de cour* of

France. Indeed the pleasure-seeking extravagance of contemporary France seemed to many Germans to provide an object-lesson in the deceptiveness of appearances. For example, we find the hero of Germany's richest seventeenth-century novel, *Simplicissimus* (1676), striking some rare good luck during his picaresque adventures as a soldier in the Thirty Years War, and heading straight for Paris with the proceeds. Before long he finds himself dubbed 'le beau alleman'. In conditions of the utmost secrecy the handsome German receives assignations to visit ladies whose nocturnal disguises are impenetrable enough to suggest to this young and complacent nonentity, this man of the people, that he has come into intimate contact with representatives of an infinitely higher sphere. The reward for such gratifying intercourse with the Olympians is a vicious bout of pox. Which leaves Simplex looking more truly like what he really was during his period of Parisian glory: a dilapidated, disgusting version of his better self. His face is no longer the face of some Grecian god, some Orpheus out of one of Poussin's paintings. It has become a caricature of the divine image. The spiritual shock is sharp, the author's purpose in this entertaining masquerade, despite appearances, solemn.

Italy, however, not France, is the setting of Germany's most searching contribution to the theme of disguise and disenchantment. The play *Cardenio und Celinde* by Andreas Gryphius was written in 1650 and first performed in the Silesian city of Breslau in 1661. Based on a Spanish story which the German poet had read in an Italian translation, its protagonist, Cardenio, is a young Spanish law student at the famous University of Bologna in Italy. Though admired by the amorous Celinde, he has fallen in love with the fair and virtuous Olympia instead; but he has lost her to his rival, Lysander, whom Olympia mistook for him when one dark night he broke into her bedchamber. Proud Cardenio has sworn to avenge this stain on his Spanish honour: lying in wait for Lysander outside his house at dead of night, he observes a veiled female figure issuing forth from it; he follows. Eventually the figure breaks its silence to tell Cardenio that she is Olympia, and that she still adores him, him alone. Meanwhile their nocturnal walk has led them into a shadowy pleasure-garden. The impulsive hero now implores Olympia to unveil herself so that he may kiss her. As she turns, unveiled, to face him, the scene is suddenly changed into a wilderness and Cardenio finds himself confronting a grinning skeleton aiming bow and arrow at him. The shock of this harrowing encounter restores him to his senses. Wishful thinking, loose desire, moral blindness have led him astray. In the starkness of that wilderness the trappings of shallow worldliness and self-indulgence fall from him. He dies a spiritual death, to be resurrected to spiritual maturity and a respect for due proportions.

The misleading appearances of others and their words, unawareness of the infinite disguises of reality: in this encounter between the student and the spectre these are revealed as marks of immaturity, and used as characteristic means of expressing the human being's natural ignorance of his own deeper identity in a perplexing world. No wonder he finds such difficulty in keeping to the straight and narrow path. Cardenio has to learn that he must reject those outward appearances by which his age seems at first sight to have set such great store, discarding them as so many masks and vain deceits deflecting his gaze from its true object, a vision of ultimate spiritual truth.

No age in modern European cultural history created a more resplendent setting in which to live. Even the poor, only watching from a distance, could enjoy the breathtaking vision of a painted church ceiling, a royal procession or a display of fireworks. Yet no age had deeper misgivings as to the ultimate value of the world in which it lived and the objects it treasured. As the baroque individual, whether king or commoner, threaded his perilous yet often glamorous way through the crowds of maskers in the piazzas of Venice, the gardens of Versailles, the pleasure-grounds of London or the streets and alleys of Madrid, in pursuit of honour, love, glory or self-indulgence, his better, more spiritual self was very prone to gaze on the labyrinth of the world and its vain pomps, and mutter some prayer like that composed by the poet Vaughan:

> Grant I may so
> Thy steps track here below,
> That in these Masques and shadows I may see
> Thy sacred way.

Behind the mask is the truth, and that truth is the divine will and plan underlying the cosmic order. Gone are the earlier days of the Jacobean revenge play with its gradual, horrific unmasking of the criminal or villain on the proverbial stage littered with corpses: retribution is no longer the order of the day. Its place is taken by the revelation of an inner meaning — of transcendental spiritual values, as in the German play *Cardenio und Celinde*, or of the transcendent quality of a prince disguised, as in *Timocrate* and so many of the operas and masques mounted in the theatres, gardens and palaces of baroque Europe.

'Savoir dissimuler est le savoir des rois', said Cardinal Richelieu, himself no mean exponent of the art, and he was echoed by the influential Spanish moralist Gracián in Aphorism 88 of his widely appreciated *Oráculo manual* (1647): 'Es gran parte de regir el disimular'. And no petty princeling or mighty potentate would ever have thought of questioning their view. Indeed the skills and arts of dissimulation, which had already been cultivated to a high degree during the Italian Renaissance, were among the first to benefit as a result of the general shift of emphasis that marked the gradual transition from the late Renaissance to the baroque.

> He who would rule so damn'd a world as this,
> Where so many dissembling villains dwell,
> Must cheat the devil, and out-dissemble hell,

blusters the ranting tyrant in John Crowne's bloodcurdling tragedy *Thyestes*, given in 1681 — or rather the ranting actor in the role. And indeed acting or putting on an act was now seen as the normal behaviour of all human beings on the stage of life. After all, prudence recommends a certain pliancy when threading the labyrinth of life, and even strict moralists were apt to consider that a degree of honest dissimulation is morally justified since it can, at times, positively help to keep and preserve that vulnerable value, truth. For ultimate truth is permanently visible only in the light of eternity. It is always subject to distortion and misrepresentation in a world whose confusing alternations of light and shadow were captured in intellectual terms by moralists such as Gracián and the Neapolitan Torquato Accetto (author of a fascinating treatise *Della dissimulazione onesta*, 1641), and in visual terms by the painter Caravaggio (1573-1610) and his numerous seventeenth-century imitators in the technique of chiaroscuro. The sharply contrasted effects of lighting, grouping and emphasis indulged in by the exponents of this school of painting such as Hendrick ter Bruggen in Utrecht and Rembrandt in Amsterdam, or Velázquez in Madrid and Murillo in Seville, provide the best visual illustration of the spiritual experiences expressed by their contemporaries, of which their paintings were often a conscious and deliberate equivalent. The theatre merely enhanced such experiences and such effects into the dimension of the histrionic. And decoration, whether it was the adornment of the individual in an attempt to conceal his true appearance, or the creation of settings appropriate to great acts of state and their fictitious counterparts on canvas or the stage, came increasingly into its own as a calling that united the aims and techniques of artist, architect, tailor and hairdresser. Italians in the main, or at least men of flair and versatility who had had their training in Italy — the master decorators, stage designers and all the other men behind the scene — played an enormous though often anonymous part in the creation and evolution of the baroque lifestyle. They were to be found in every court and city of Europe, finally penetrating even distant Muscovy: men like Inigo Jones (1573-1652), the principal British exponent of an essentially baroque phenomenon, whose lasting monument is the Italianate Piazza at Covent Garden, but whose contemporary celebrity was acquired by the series of court masques which he designed between 1605 and 1613, in Shakespeare's lifetime, that is, yet conveying a flavour which is baroque rather than Elizabethan. The cult of decorative effects and aesthetic deception inaugurated in England by Inigo Jones, and being much more fully developed in other parts of Europe, was to reach its peaks in the 1630s and then in the 1660s, in two great flowerings of baroque culture separated from each other by a period of starker realism, austerity, even violent upheaval.

Later, towards the end of the seventeenth century, there was to be another return to the fashion for masquerade; but it was rarified now in the more brittle atmosphere of late baroque and early rococo. Sometimes the mood was one of nostalgia as captured in the dreamy paintings of Watteau, or of Venetian decline as seen in the serene Adriatic light of a Canaletto. Or sometimes it was the icy brilliance of drawing-room comedy as represented in England by Congreve, whose *Double-Dealer* of 1693 turns on the intrigues of its dissembling villain, the aptly named Maskwell. But there are no apotheoses here, and no sudden revelations of the supernatural or the divine:

> No mask like open truth to cover lies,
> As to go naked is the best disguise,

declares Congreve's comic rogue on the eve of the eighteenth-century Enlightenment — as if to go naked were the next thing to going invisible! The mask has turned into an elegant toy, and unmasking is reduced to little more than an effective comic dénouement. When such trivializations occur, it is a sure sign that the baroque, with all its searching paradoxes and tensions, is no more.

3

Nymphs & shepherds

'Nymphs and Shepherds, come away, come away, in these Groves
let's sport and play. . .' To Purcell's music the invitation echoes on,
while the visual imagination, roused by memories of gardens real or
evoked on the walls and ceilings of painted rooms, catches a
glimpse of the fleeting train of scantily clad figures as they move off
in answer to its exhortation into some landscape of meadow, brook
and copse bathed in the golden sunlight of an exquisite and eternal
evening. Where do they come from, these figures too real to be
forgotten, yet too intangible ever to be met in everyday reality?
And what is the significance of the charmed world they inhabit — a
domain too blissful for us to dismiss out of hand with the disdainful
indifference of wiser posterity?

All over baroque Europe that fragile world left its lasting
impression. Not only was it given shape and form in graceful
statuary and ornamental painting. Its imagined contours and
enchanting vistas were re-created in countless settings, from the
relatively modest grounds of country gentlemen to the sumptuous
parks of princes; and it is wise to remember that some of the former
still exist when marvelling at the larger-scale evocations of an
imaginary world at, say, the Nymphenburg, aptly named summer
residence of the Electors of Bavaria outside Munich, or in the
breathtaking cascades which embellish the grounds of the kings of
the Two Sicilies at Caserta, near Naples, among which the goddess
Diana is for ever taking her revenge on the amorous huntsman

Acteon by turning him into a stag to be devoured by his own hounds. Is this really nature not yet debauched by art? Is not the pastoral world of the baroque no more than a concerted attempt at escapism — an attempt in landscape-gardening, in painting or in literature to deflect the gaze from the rigours of reality? For in those days life was harsh enough because of disease and ignorance, and was often made harsher still by the carnage and brutality of the innumerable wars which laid waste whole countrysides. And these no amount of martial pomp could entirely glamourize, since those who fought and died in them were those same princes and gentlemen whose taste encouraged pastoral escape. Diana's hunt tears baying through these woods. It is at once a remote mythological allusion and a significant metaphor: the note of violence could never be entirely contained. In the first of Virgil's *Eclogues* the shepherd Meliboeus is forced by Rome's civil wars to leave his beloved woodlands and pastures while Tityrus continues to enjoy the tranquil charms of his. And the example of Virgil, together with the idyllic verse of Theocritus and Propertius, was to re-echo in this modern age which none the less still read Greek and Latin and saw itself as a confirmation and fulfilment of antiquity. What then appears at first no more than escapism is in fact a major instance of the revitalization of an old and rich tradition. No wonder that these nymphs and shepherds, when they strike us as most baroque, are apt to turn out to be modelled often very closely on Greek or Latin originals, whether in the visual arts or in poetry.

An age as acutely conscious of classical precedents as the late Renaissance can be forgiven for having prided itself on inventing one artistic form which the ancients might have had but never did. Such was the claim the Italian poet Giambattista Guarini (1538-1612) made for his pastoral tragicomedy *Il Pastor Fido*. The adventures of lovelorn swains and chaste shepherdesses had become the favourite reading of courtly and aristocratic circles in Western Europe ever since the romance of the shepherdess Diana by Jorge de Montemayor had captivated Spanish society in 1559 and the delights of *Daphnis and Chloe*, most famous surviving ancient Greek pastoral love story, had been rediscovered by French readers in a translation of the same year. Both these novels were indeed to retain their popularity throughout the baroque period and, together with a host of lesser imitations and variations, they provided a constant and living tradition to which reading fashions in various countries repeatedly and profitably returned. Yet with Guarini's *Faithful Shepherd* (1589) a new world opened up, full of possibilities and the intimations of new modes of feeling and expression; soon Europe was enthralled. It may be harder in the twentieth century to understand what people then so obviously saw in it; yet the fact remains that few works of literature have ever achieved such widespread and prolonged popularity. Countless editions of the original poured from the printing presses of Italy, and translations of it proliferated; sixty-four, it is said, in all, with ten into Dutch alone during the course of the seventeenth century. In beguiling and revealing words the Italian poet stated that his aim was to convey 'the delight, but not the sadness; the danger, not the death', and it was surely this, expressed with what his readers regarded as incomparable poetic beauty, which carried *Il Pastor Fido* into the very front rank of European literature throughout the baroque age.

For here, surely, we have the most direct and the most eloquent exposition of the baroque attitude towards the poetry of love and that whole realm of the profane and the erotic of which it was so jubilantly, indeed licentiously aware. The delights and the dangers of love are ultimately the sole and sufficient subject of baroque love poetry; and the closer the proximity of peril and pleasure, the intenser the excitement, and the more dazzling the effect. The sadness, meanwhile, and the death had been the theme of some of the most intense and most elegiac of the love poems of Petrarch or of the Pléiade poets in sixteenth-century France and the great Elizabethans — that great and already very rich lyric tradition which was the background against which the baroque poets had consciously to work, and of which the lyrics with which the Spanish *Diana* is interspersed were one of the best-known expressions.

> Quello è vero gioire,
> Che nasce da virtù dopo il soffrire

the chorus proclaims in the last lines of Guarini's universally popular pastoral tragicomedy. 'True joy is a thing that springs from Vertue after suffering': this is the pleasurable lesson learnt by Mirtillo, the 'faithful shepherd', who was ready to die for the beautiful maiden Amarilli and who, after many vicissitudes, is rewarded with her hand in sylvan marriage in accordance with the words of an oracle, words on which the whole delightful and confusing action turns:

> Your Woe shall end when two of Race Divine
>   Love shall combine:
> And for a faithlesse Nymph's apostate state
> A Faithfull Shepherd supererogate.

But what is love? What faithfulness? The old-accepted and indeed conventional terms of European love poetry and its attendant ideals and conventions — terms that recur throughout the rambling romances and countless sonnets of the preceding period — were in *Il Pastor Fido* resuscitated and presented with a freshness that gave its readers an impression of novelty. Such revitalizations of the accepted and jejune were to be a characteristic of much baroque art; and never were they so striking and successful as when they cast new light on a tradition, on conventions very old indeed and going back beyond the Renaissance, and beyond Petrarch even, to antiquity. The actual appearance of Guarini's play is itself symptomatic of this: with its choruses, set speeches and dialogues, its mythological allusions and its deliberate similarities to a great Renaissance model, Tasso's pastoral *Aminta*, it challenged the assumptions of its day. To the reader of Renaissance literature it looks derivative, and indeed it often is; yet it opened up fresh fields and pastures new and evoked amidst them a vision of the Golden Age — already over, or yet to come, who could tell? — in contrast to a present which seventeenth-century man would only too readily recognize, since it was expressed in his age's most characteristic terms, a Golden Age when

> That pompous sound, Idoll of vanity,
> Made up of Title, Pride, and Flattery,
> Which they call Honour whom Ambition blindes,
> Was not as yet the Tyrant of our mindes,
> But to buy reall goods with honest toil
> Amongst the woods and flocks, to use no guile,
> Was honour to those sober souls that knew
> No happiness but what from vertue grew.

The capital letters used in Sir Richard Fanshawe's brilliant translation of 1647 are eloquent in themselves: the translator made the relevance to the contemporary world even more explicit when he told his dedicatee, the future Charles II, that Guarini in 'exposing to *ordinary view* an Enterlude of shepherds, their loves, and other little concernments, with the stroke of a lighter pencil, presents through the *perspective* of the *Chorus*, another and more suitable object to his *Royall Spectators*. He shews to *them* the image of a *gasping state.*' To the discriminating reader, pastoral antics could provide much more than a diversion or an invitation to escapism, by bringing home the contrasts between their world and his.

The contrast between bold incontinence and the gentler power of chaste austerity had been presented some ten years before Fanshawe's translation of Guarini appeared. The most celebrated English contribution to the fashion for pastoral dramatics, Milton's masque *Comus*, was first presented at Ludlow Castle in 1634 and published in 1637, just before the young poet set off for Italy. It lacks all the dramatic expertise and psychological coherence of its great Italian forerunner, yet in another way comes very close to it, for its language reflects to an extraordinary degree the ornate limpidity of the Italian written by Guarini and the many other pastoral and elegiac poets of Italy — a language brought to such a high degree of poetic sophistication and polish that it wears all the ease of casual conversation, but the conversation of a highly educated and elegant society. Milton was of course building on a tradition in English poetry going back to Elizabethans such as Spenser and Sidney; English, too, was highly wrought and well established as the poetic intercourse of a civilized and courtly minority. Yet such was the delicacy of his ear, and such his ability to translate the conventions of his imaginary world into actual English words, that we have in *Comus*, and in the *Arcades* and *Lycidas*, the definitive evocation of the baroque pastoral landscape and its inhabitants in our language. Thus it was that the most competently Italianate of our seventeenth-century poets did indeed fulfil what was to be expected of him: the soft pipe and the smooth-dittied song, those gently Mediterranean sounds of the new Arcadia, re-echoed here in the sequestered nooks and solitudes of an English landscape.

The cultural process here described does in fact no more than echo what Guarini had expressed in the Prologue to his *Il Pastor Fido*. There, in the pleasing form of an extended metaphor, the river Alpheus, which used to flow through the benign landscape of the original Arcadia in ancient Greece, wells up among the vales and woods of the new Italy, having made its way beneath the ocean in amorous pursuit of its beloved, the nymph Arethusa. And here,

in late sixteenth-century Italy, it rediscovers the sweet land of
Arcady: here, now, it finds again the fortunate landscape where
once virtue dwelt: here, in this corner of the contemporary world, it
seems that the Golden Age might live again, for it was here that
'the golden age retired when she her flight had took from sinfull
men'. Arcadia translated, Arcady refound, was henceforth to
become a major theme in pastoral poetry, itself often little more
than a translation into words of what the baroque age was creating
in its parks and gardens, and in its paintings, on a scale majestically
vast or intimately small.

The echoes of this mythical pastoral world, be they the love songs
of amorous swains or the laments for nymphs or shepherds
presumed or really dead, were to become an insistently recurring
feature of baroque poetry, and of its music too. The affinities
between the two were at their closest in the area of pastoral lament
and love song, for here the concept of the lyric was being restored to
what was imagined by theorists to have been its original harmony in
far-off classical days. The madrigal writing of the later sixteenth
century, spreading throughout Europe in countless complex patterns of influence and reciprocal imitation, established in the minds
of cultivated people an awareness of the lyric as an intertwining of
poetic and musical voices imitating and echoing one another with
increasing daring and effectiveness until, in the music of Monteverdi especially, the echo became an essential feature in its own
right, as it did in the many so-called echo-poems of his period. Not
only was a word or sound echoed for simple musical or sylvan effect;
with growing sophistication baroque poets and musicians began to
delight in the subtler possibilities of this pastoral speciality. The
abandoned nymph, the lovelorn swain, that is, the isolated human
voice, the individual human being, began to find their joys or
laments not just echoed by surrounding nature but re-echoed
meaningfully: that is, the final syllables of a phrase would be
repeated in such a way that they formed a disembodied yet valid
comment on it. Thus the inanimate itself became endowed with
voice in sympathetic response to a single mortal's audible expression of his inmost feelings. This could be, and often was, no more
than an opportunity for elegant displays of poetic cleverness or
musicianly craftsmanship. But sometimes, in moments of intensity,
it could be suggestive of infinitely more, and bring to mind old
theories concerning the arcane theology that underlies the poet's

song, or notions of a cosmic harmony. But, whichever the case, this general delight in the aesthetic possibilities of the echo brings home one of the essential characteristics of the baroque, and one that is perhaps more easily discernible in architecture, painting or music than in poetry. And this is its handling of a new and exciting dimension — space. It is no coincidence that the age between Galileo's telescope (1609) and the establishment of the Royal Observatory (1676) was also the great age of antiphonal choruses in sacred music and echo effects in profane song, and of the vast ceilings opening up into painted skies in the churches and chambers in which they were sung.

It was in France, however, that the most important translation of the pastoral ideals of Arcadia to a new landscape took place. Few books exerted a more pervasive influence on this whole aspect of baroque Europe, and few of its great works have fallen into more general oblivion than the vast novel which a French country gentleman took to composing in his leisure, to find to our amazement that he had wandered upon the secret all writers covet: that of bestselling success. *L'Astrée* by Honoré d'Urfé (1567-1625) began to appear in 1607, further volumes following at intervals in 1610, 1619 and 1627. Its length was enormous, and its public devoured it with elegant rapacity, sighing for a final consummation and dénouement which in a sense could never be forthcoming, for *L'Astrée*, culmination of the Renaissance pastoral novel and model for the entire baroque age in Europe, was in its strange way a reflection of life itself. Its imaginary world mirrored reality sufficiently well for that reflection to be recognizable and very meaningful to contemporary readers. Like the courtly romances of the Middle Ages and their successor, *Amadis de Gaule*, which had played a similarly influential part throughout the sixteenth century, *L'Astrée* was concerned with love first and above all else; but it was a new interpretation of the many faces of love carried out in endless protractions and in a new and evocatively pastoral setting. Its whole vast edifice turns on the play of the three French words *aimer — amer — animer*: its innumerable strands, entwined with a complexity which beguiled readers then and bewilders them now, all examine and illuminate the fundamental equations implicit in those words. Is love essentially an experience which leaves a bitter taste? Or is love ultimately the animating force which brings all nature, and with it the human heart, to life? Like faithfulness and

valour, twin virtues that both inevitably proceed from it, love in
L'Astrée is a motive force, an emotion which entails total rejection
of that central notion of all classicism whether ancient, Renaissance
or eighteenth-century: the 'golden mean'. In love there can be no
moderation, no excess; for in this pastoral philosophy it is absolute,
and has absolute claims to make. It is a flame which burns with
such singleminded purity that it has no smoke; a fire that blazes
with a heat so white, it cannot burn. For all the obvious influence of
Platonic philosophy here and of its revived Renaissance variations,
it is clear that the theme of d'Urfé's novel is above all else a profane
and primarily entertaining equivalent of that new singleminded-
ness of purpose and total self-commitment which informs both the
militancy and the mysticism of the baroque period's regenerate
Christianity. It proved to be, if the analogy is not too daring, the
holy writ of that other modish plane of existence, the vicarious life
of the pastoral world. Astrée, its remote and virginal heroine,
provided an ideal of womankind to be adored and worshipped from
afar; and its shepherd hero, Céladon, soon became the universal
pattern and epitome of fidelity and undemanding love, with whom
all young men of taste and quality could identify, right down to his
garb of pale bluish green. France and soon much of Europe, intent
on developing a civilized style of life, had good reason to be
grateful to d'Urfé for having given such full and explicit guidance
on how to keep man's supreme emotion in such decorously
stimulating check.

In another way, too, L'Astrée can be seen as symptomatic of the
times. Its grandiose concealment or sublimation of personal experience went hand in hand with a remarkable attempt not just to
translate Arcady to a new setting, but to come closer to the particular qualities of a specific place. Pastoral writing had always been
fired by the experience of love and had always delighted in evoking
imaginary settings perfectly suited to its imagined enjoyment. But
now this was superseded by the discovery of truly Arcadian
landscapes nearer home. Perhaps this development was a natural
conseqence of the gradual emergence of the concept of the national
state during the sixteenth century. At all events d'Urfé, in selecting
his own area of Forez in Central France as his Arcadia, was on a
grand scale doing very much what Drayton did in his topographical
poem Poly-Olbion (1612, 1622) and what Germany's leading poet
of that period, Martin Opitz, was to do for his native Silesia in the

first, much briefer, German pastoral, *The Nymph Hercinia* (1630): that is, he was successfully introducing a patriotic element by making the Arcadian setting a source of national satisfaction or at least provincial pride. Sabrina fair, rising attended by water nymphs, in Milton's masque written for Ludlow Castle, is a slight but eloquent example of a widespread turn to the make-believe worship of local divinities, and to a genuine love of brave and ancient things.

It was of course largely for this reason that the baroque pastoral writers secured wide readership among the landed gentry and aristocracy of Europe, from whose ranks they often came. The traditionally close links between the pastoral and the georgic — that is, didactic poetry on the arts and pleasures of husbandry — reflected the realities of their life while giving it a patina of elegance and erudition, and confirmed many a European gentleman in his desire or duty to mind his own estates and keep himself outside the perilous whirlpools of court life, with its intrigue and expense, and its threats to life, reputation and morals. The humble cottage in preference to the palace: this old and hackneyed classical topos took on new and immediate meaning in every European country at various times during the baroque period, and is therefore a common feature of all its art in the broadly pastoral mode; it was never more frequent than during the period of disaffection between nobility and central royal government discernible in many parts of Europe between 1640 and 1660.

If pastoral exerted a beneficial influence on the country pursuits of the aristocracy, or at least reflected their growing interest in such a way of life, the decision of Louis XIV to move his court from central Paris to the erstwhile hunting lodge of Versailles displays a grandiose and bold attempt to identify cottage with palace and thereby create a new pattern of court life in a majestically pastoral setting. The trend inaugurated by the French king was imitated far and wide, especially by the princelings of the innumerable states into which the Holy Roman Empire was divided. Country palaces and mansions sprang up everywhere during the last decades of the century and well on into the next and — what is just as important though more easy to overlook in retrospect — vast estates were organized and laid out around them, in which scenic beauty afforded an idyllic setting for pastoral entertainment and the pleasures of the chase. Indeed the sounds of the hunt echoed across

Europe unless they were drowned by the brasher din of war; in baroque Europe the huntress Diana, chaste and fair, reigned supreme, her sway disturbed only by the protracted loves of Mars and Venus locked in amorous combat. The mythology was meaningful indeed.

In France especially, but in many other countires too which looked increasingly to France as arbiter of taste and fashion, the civilizing influences emanating from *L'Astrée* and its like were greater still. Much of the novel's vast and rambling text was taken up with protracted discussions among the lovesick swains and shepherdesses, a feature already established by its chief precursor, the Spanish *Diana* of Montemayor, and these discussions turned on the finer points of personal conduct and emotional self-analysis. Society devoured them, read them in the isolation and leisure of a country estate, and put their advice into practice back at court; and so it came about that the pastoral novel both reflected and gave added impetus to the establishment of an ideal of politeness in the domains of manners and social intercourse. It laid the greatest stress on self-scrutiny, while at the same time encouraging the intimately social arts of gallantry, flirtation and lovemaking within the well-defined limits of pastoral convention. Because of its fashionable appeal, the bounds of decorum set by the pastoral novel formed a powerful yet elegant bulwark against the baroque age's otherwise compulsive propensities towards licentiousness and even coarseness; for the lustful satyr too is a traditional inhabitant of Arcadia, always lurking in the background and ready to disgrace it if given the chance. Significantly, perhaps, such satyrical propensities were more overtly apparent in England or Germany than in Louis XIV's France or in that of his father. Here under Louis XIII, the very rigour of these decorous restrictions gave society opportunity for liberation within conventions, and for an enormous expansion in the range of amorous intercourse reflected in the famous salons of the period such as that of the Hôtel de Rambouillet, which occupied a commanding position in polite society between 1630 and 1645, and radiated its sophisticated, often exquisite influence far and wide during the period, famous prototype of countless long-forgotten imitations.

Should the rarified atmosphere that prevailed in such circles be taken seriously? Much of their success was due to fashion; much of their sophistication shallow and little more than affectation.

Extravagance and preciousness marked much of their behaviour and their artistic productions, and both these features represented distortions of the ideals they thought they were upholding. There is much hollowness here, and much artificiality. Yet it is the hollowness and artificiality of an art, a culture and a way of life above all aware of the essential confusion of appearance and reality. The result might often be itself confused, and the emphasis mistaken; but to overlook it because its affectation and artificiality are distasteful is to fail to come to terms with an essential quality of the baroque which first emerged with clarity during the 1630-40 decade.

The cultural experience of that decade and the various traditions that led up to it was of course recorded by many artists working in different media. But there were two painters who succeeded in capturing its central qualities in particularly effective ways: Rubens and Poussin. Both excelled in the pastoral mode, but each represents a distinct and complementary aspect of it. About 1632 Rubens completed his *Feast of Venus* (Vienna, Kunsthistorisches Museum), an exuberant canvas in which nymphs, satyrs and putti dance in abandon round a living statue of the goddess of love, before whom a cloud of incense rises, vivid pointer towards the high-baroque shift of emphasis away from decorum towards the explicitly and jubilantly erotic, which was to culminate in the theme of 'all for love'. Meanwhile a spring, a temple, flowing water to the left, not seen at first, provide suggestive counterpoint: the amorous abandon of the moment, its cult of beauty and its adoration of love are as endlessly recurring as life itself, and just as evanescent. Poussin, in the meantime, was producing his two versions of the pastoral theme 'Et in Arcadia Ego'. The first, at Chatsworth and dating from 1629-30, depicts two shepherds and a shepherdess discovering a rustic altar in a calmly sylvan setting. The Latin words are carved upon it, but of this they seem almost as oblivious as of the rugged river-god reclining symbolically in the right foreground. In his second version (*c.* 1640, Paris, Louvre) the changes are significant. The mortal beings are apparently attempting to decipher the arcane inscription on the altar — or is it some forgotten tomb? Upon it lies a skull, at which the earlier painting only hinted: the river-god has vanished. Does the title mean, as some have thought, that once another shepherd also dwelt in fortunate Arcadia? Or does it mean that death itself is as much an inevitable presence in this charmed idyllic world as it is in the world of our reality? Be that as it may; what is significant about these two great paintings is that each captures the vital present moment in the receding vista and flux of time, and that each concentrates on one of the two supreme forces which to the baroque imagination are omnipresent and all-pervasive: love and death. Without time, love and death, the pastoral world can no more exist than can the world we live in, of which Arcady with all its nymphs and shepherds was but an extended metaphor or enhanced reflected image.

4

Martyrs & virgins

What is a mask, and where is the truth? These questions reflect a theme that underlies the baroque in Europe: not so much its music and its painting as its poetry and, above all, its drama, where alone the ambiguities of human motivation and the paradoxes surrounding thought and action could be displayed and analysed in dialogue and soliloquy, in roles assumed and identities revealed.

Ultimate truth is the revealed truth of religion: of this the age was universally convinced. And man is an actor on the stage of life: of this it was equally certain. And it also knew full well that death is the inevitable dénouement of the play of life however well or ill constructed, and that it is death too which will finally reveal that ultimate truth sought or rejected by proud, vainglorious man as he leads his fugitive life against a backdrop of eternity. In the face of death the mask will fall; tragedy must therefore clearly be the art form best suited to the revelation of truth to a living audience.

On one occasion the possibilities of this situation were seized in their extremest form and concentrated in the single action of a play that is one of the masterpieces of the baroque period. *Le Véritable Saint-Genest* was modelled on various Jesuit and Spanish forerunners by Rotrou, a successful French playwright, in 1647; in its fascinating handling of its material it remains a representative yet unique theatrical experience. Genest is an actor in ancient Rome. He is summoned to appear before the pagan emperor Diocletian (and his victorious general Maximin) to give a performance of his finest role: that of the Christian martyr Adrien. But on this occasion fiction merges with reality. The actor assumes not just the part of Adrien; he assumes his faith, and in a climax of extreme tragic effectiveness casts his mask aside and to the applause of his imperial audience acts out the supreme dénouement of his play, the martyr's death, in earnest. The actor's triumph was a martyr's death: the actor's martyrdom is the dead man's triumph. And as Rotrou audaciously equated mime and martyr by celebrating sacred wonders on the profane Parisian stage, he unambiguously declared one thing at least: his age's innate and irrepressible passion for the theatre and its unique capacity for setting forth its values and its view of life.

The exaltation of martyrdom for the faith was in fact to become a major and central concern of the baroque world. Here it could discharge some of that pent-up energy which the fashionable refinement of conduct and the emotions was tending to tone down. Here, too, the continuing momentum of the Counter-Reformation could manifest itself in a manner so intensely dramatic that it is hard to believe that later ages could so easily and often fail to appreciate its intrinsic verve and vitality. The Jesuits led the way: Latin plays formed an important part of their proselytizing mission wherever the Society of Jesus was allowed to carry out its activities in public, and so in almost all countries outside England and Scandinavia audiences were made graphically aware of the vicissitudes the pious Christian must expect to undergo and the glorious prize awaiting him as his oppressors are cast into hideous and eternal torment. Such plays provided the cosmopolitan foundation on which in various places more localized vernacular adaptations of the theme arose. Nor are these as independent of each other as one might first think, for here too the essentially international character of the baroque was decisive.

Today the best known of these dramatic variations on the glorious theme of martyrdom for the Christian faith is Pierre Corneille's tragedy *Polyeucte*, first played in 1643 (the year of Louis XIV's accession). Polyeucte's fame is due not only to Corneille's lasting eminence as one of France's favourite playwrights. It is also because no other European martyr drama is at once so controlled and orderly in outward appearance and yet so fraught with far-reaching, perhaps ultimately insoluble problems. It is of course one of those plays which go to make up the French classical repertory. Its formal precision and measured diction may indeed seem to exclude it from the strictly baroque, since form and measure, together with constant attention to detail and consistency of plot and motivation, are the standards by which critics and theorists in France strove to attain a classical norm and ward off the alluring but aesthetically and morally perilous seductions of the dominant artistic trend in Europe at the time. But to these seductions Corneille was himself not immune. Thus we find from the outset in this great play a tension which only his supremely disciplined yet imaginatively creative mind could turn to positive dramatic advantage; for it is transposed into the domains of private emotions and personal religious convictions.

Polyeucte, an Armenian gentleman attracted to the new religion of Christ, is married to Pauline, the beautiful daughter of that province's Roman governor, who in turn has had to renounce her earlier love for a chivalrous Roman, Sévère. Tensions religious and emotional thus lie concealed just beneath the calm of the play's opening, disturbed only by a dream that has troubled Pauline's slumber; but they are tensions heading with increasing momentum for a double showdown, for while Polyeucte is making up his mind to commit himself once and for all to his new-found faith, Sévère emerges from Pauline's past, successful, attractive and still in love. Idealism, glamour, loyalty and tenderness: these people are all so highminded, their intentions are so admirable, their conduct so courteous — yet their tragedy is ineluctable nevertheless. And the decisive action, when it occurs, strikes like nearby lightning. For suddenly an action offstage brings all these fair words, these civilized exchanges, to a point of crisis. To demonstrate private commitment by public action, Polyeucte commits the unthinkable. He destroys the statue of the pagan Jupiter in his very sanctuary. The pious vandalism of this highminded hero is an act only fully comprehensible, perhaps, in an age whose churches so often resembled the temples of Roman antiquity. To pious Catholic French contemporaries Polyeucte's desecration of a pagan temple surely struck with the full force of modern Protestantism, yet paradoxically Polyeucte is none other than an exemplary Christian hero rushing towards martyrdom to demonstrate his — and their — personal faith. And so the polite, measured world of moderation and harmony is upset: there is no place in it for the immoderate yet saintly claims Polyeucte advances in his celebrated third-act dialogue with Pauline, and which clearly touch on familiar themes:

> Worldly greatness will perish: I want immortality,
> To be sure of a happiness boundless and endless,
> Far above envy, far above fate.
> To procure it is surely worth a sad life
> Which any day, suddenly, may be snatched from me,
> Which can only offer a fleeting moment of happiness,
> And cannot guarantee that another will follow?

The issues here are typical and the argument persuasive: it comes as a surprise which is no real surprise when Pauline a second time renounces the man who merely deserves her affection and embraces the faith of the hero to whom she is married, ready to rush with him to the glory of martyrdom. Celestial truth or wilful blindness? 'I see,' she cries; 'I know; I believe; and I have lost my illusions!' As she utters these words, we continue to wonder whether she has woken up from a dream or whether she is in the grips of one, for dreaming and waking pervade this whole play. But when every character has aroused admiration, to wonder thus at the end is enough to justify the play's inclusion.

To his fellow Frenchmen, Corneille's martyr tragedy seemed an unquestionable contribution to the new cult of the exemplary and unblemished hero: a hero who possessed not only the classical pagan virtues of fortitude and self-discipline but in addition exulted in the Christian virtues too. But to Andreas Gryphius, a German poet of sombre yet sensitive outlook and Lutheran background, it raised questions which he resolved to challenge in a martyr tragedy of his own. Superficially similar and almost identical in date, the German play takes us into a very different world in its quest for a suitable way of exalting martyrdom for the faith in dramatically effective terms. Set in contemporary Persia, its action was based on a recent event — *Catharina von Georgien* centres on a noble heroine: a Caucasian queen held captive by the Shah. Unshakable in her faith and virtuous in her personal conduct, this admirable woman unintentionally succeeds in arousing the Moslem monarch's love. Transient prospects of deliverance scarcely disturb the central vista of this drama, which is that in the end Catharina will go meekly yet majestically to her doom, her only true release, and thereby win the martyr's eternal crown. The Shah, caught for his part in the trammels of this dark world below, will only find that his senseless attempts to save and possess his adored victim ultimately lead him to destroy her and to be destroyed in turn by the triumphant reassertion of a passion now for ever unattainable, a paradox that drives him finally into that living hell, despair. In marked contrast to the French play, where all the resources of dramatic technique are elegantly and excitingly brought into operation to achieve an action that accelerates towards a climax at once convincing and worthy of admiration, here, in its German counterpart, the aim is to sustain excitement throughout a situation which, though prolonged, is majestically, almost ponderously, static. The two poles of believer and unbeliever, of cruel tyrant and helpless victim, of sensuous lover and virginal heroine, remain constant while continuously generating intense poetic argument, the argument between spiritual freedom and sensual captivity, over and across the unbridgeable gulf fixed between them.

The moral, spiritual and sexual antinomies that constitute the drama are moreover contained within a frame which gives them a graphic eschatological dimension: death, judgement, heaven and hell — these are prospects at once timeless and typical of the time in which the play was written and performed. It opens with a memorable and awesome prologue which is a perfect verbal equivalent of those tombs of the Jacobean and Caroline periods in England and of the baroque in Europe: tombs whose startlingly frank depictions of mortality — decomposing corpses, grinning skulls, broken columns, mourning cherubs — are to be found standing black and white in the silence of churches everywhere where the baroque left its tangible and visible mark. From heaven above, Eternity, an allegorical figure, descends on to a stage strewn with corpses and the discarded insignia of earthly glory, underneath which Hell itself gapes open, and in majestically portentous lines proclaims to the awestruck audience that this, the stage, is her domain: choose, mortals, choose! But if your choice be wrong, nothing on this earth can help you. Gaze upon the bliss of heaven: here is joy and consolation! On the dungeons of damnation: here is nought but tribulation! Highest joy or lamentation — which is it to be? This is what can make or mar you for eternity! And so the whole audience, the whole of humanity is drawn into the play and summoned to make a choice: to choose between the Shah or Catherine.

The original St Catherine, martyred on her famous wheel that was to become a favourite firework, is the subject of the most far-fetched and dazzling of these martyr plays, which, between them, give a clear indication of the scope covered by this peculiarly baroque speciality. Dryden's *Tyrannic Love; or, The Royal Martyr* was produced in 1669, when he was at the height of his most histrionically baroque phase and intent on developing an English repertory which would take over something of the sophisticated brilliance and heroic bravado of contemporary French literature while also gratifying the taste of the volatile audiences of Restoration London. The resultant pursuit of intellectual cleverness coupled with unabashed, larger-than-life theatricality led in his hands to a type of stage entertainment which has not found much favour in England since, but certainly represents a valid and enjoyable extension of European drama if seen in the context of the baroque. Like *Catharina von Georgien*, *Tyrannic Love* dramatizes irreconcilable opposites to great effect: Christian virtue, self-confident and heaven-bent, in its saintly heroine, and undisciplined worldly passion in Maximin, the bloody Roman tyrant whose captive the virgin martyr is. He, of course, attempts to win his beautiful and otherworldly captive's love; 'There's not a God ... but for this Christian would all heaven forswear,' he exclaims with hyperbolic irony. But there is no common ground between saint and despot, only grounds for a curiously exciting blend of theological and erotic argument in which all the figures in the play become caught up, and which generates an excitement of an entirely baroque kind.

They may be nothing more than puppets danced upon the wire of Dryden's flamboyant imagination, these figures with their exuberant protestations of undying love and inordinate passion. Yet the presence of St Catherine herself in the whirlpool of this far-fetched world brings home something of the paradoxical quality of the baroque age, which could produce a work containing opposites so violently juxtaposed yet giving an integrated impression none the less. And this is because the virgin heroine is herself conceived in flamboyant terms. Intent on gaining a martyr's crown, she is still sufficiently human to admit

> Were there no sting in death, for me to die,
> Would not be conquest, but stupidity.

And indeed the prospect of martyrdom is conveyed with much of the quasi-erotic sadism for which Dryden's German contemporaries, Gryphius and Lohenstein, were renowned:

Maximin. Go, bind her hand and foot beneath that wheel.
        Four of you turn the dreadful engine round;
        Four others hold her fastened to the ground;
        That, by degrees, her tender breasts may feel,
        First, the rough razings of the pointed steel;
        Her paps then let the bearded tenters stake,
        And on each hook a gory gobbet take;
        Till the upper flesh, by piece-meal torn away,
        Her beating heart shall to the sun display.

But faith is a 'force from which there's no defence', because it has a
vision of a future life behind the pangs of death. 'To minds
resolved, the threat of death is vain', as Maximin discovers. To
Catherine it is a plunge into eternity: one moment ends our pain.
So, in ecstatic mood, she can declaim:

        No streak of blood (the relics of the earth)
        Shall stain my soul in her immortal birth;
        But she shall mount all pure, a white and virgin mind,
        And full of all that peace, which there she goes to find.

So, in the end, it is the exaltation of martyrdom, not its horror, that
calls forth the most tellingly baroque passage in *Tyrannic Love*. As
its virgin heroine is led off to die, English too proves itself capable
of that 'pious madness' which informs both the baroque martyr
play and the minds of those men who built, worshipped and made
music in the ornately imposing churches dedicated to their spiritual
heroes and heroines:

        Betwixt her guards she seem'd by bride-men led,
        Her cheeks with cheerful blushes were o'erspread;
        When, smiling, to the axe she bow'd her head,
        Just at the stroke,
        Aetherial music did her breath prepare,
        Like joyful sounds of spousals in the air;
        A radiant light did her crown'd temples gild,
        And all the place with fragrant scents was fill'd;
        The balmy mist came thickening to the ground,
        And sacred silence cover'd all around.

If Dryden's martyr play rings splendid but untrue, this is chiefly
because his was an attempt to create an effect rather than to give

voice to deep-felt moral and spiritual convictions such as were held
by Gryphius. The German's tragedy was the product of searing
experience and of the tensions which racked Germany during the
appallingly destructive campaigns of the Thirty Years War, and
which were carried by the continuing struggle between Protestantism
and Counter-Reformation right into his native province of Silesia,
which had largely escaped the warfare. *Tyrannic Love*, like all
Dryden's heroic plays, is by contrast an expression of relief after the
tensions of Civil War and Commonwealth, written when commitment to an abstract cause was no longer a serious issue, as James II
was to discover, when he tried to introduce the Counter-
Reformation into England, only to be ousted ingloriously in the
'bloodless' revolution of 1688. No, commitment in Restoration
England was rather an articulate but hollow pose carrying little of
the burning conviction it still commanded especially in Central
Europe when, after 1648, peace was finally restored. Here energetic
Jesuit proselytizing expansion, in every way comparable with its
better-known manifestations in Latin America and the Far East,
had in some way to be reconciled with the claims and aspirations of
the whole community, itself in large measure Protestant. No
wonder the Rome of Maximin and Catherine, or of Polyeucte and
Pauline, tended to take on a more immediate and different
colouring as the complex epitome of both contemporary Catholicism and differing notions of imperial destiny. In the exuberant
splendour of Roman triumphs, private differences could be to a
large extent submerged; and imperial Vienna, capital of the Holy
Roman Empire, now began to witness a succession of baroque
spectacles on a scale of hitherto unimagined lavishness and ostentation. Like the English heroic plays, or indeed the plays of the
early years of Louis XIV's personal reign (from 1661 on), these too
represented a feeling of general relief and of stability regained. But
it was a relief with a very definite political and social purpose: to
rediscover the living tradition of Central European unity in a blend
of religious fervour, patriotic purpose and sensual excitement.

It was during the fitful lull that preceded Charles II's Restoration, while Tumble Down Dick was feebly trying to prolong his
father's Protectorate, and on the eve of Louis XIV's assumption of
personal power, that these Viennese spectacles reached an unparalleled degree of splendour to mark the accession, in 1658, of
Leopold I, the fiftieth ruler of the Holy Roman Empire. Short of

stature and monumentally ugly, Leopold of Habsburg was not brought up as the heir to a throne and had lived solely for religion, art and music. But the death of an elder brother compelled him, like Charles I of England, reluctantly to assume an exalted office which he held for the next forty-seven years, till 1705. This of course makes him the closest counterpart as well as the lifelong opponent of Louis XIV, and, though much less famous outside Austria and Germany, we should remember that he too was one of the exemplary monarchs of the baroque age. Leopold's reign was inaugurated by a display which epitomizes the baroque as it appeared in Central Europe. Before some 3000 spectators and in the illustrious presence of the emperor and his court, the Jesuit College in Vienna staged the most memorable of what were known as the *ludi caesarei* or imperial plays. Composed by Nicolaus von Avancini, its professor of rhetoric and philosophy, *Pietas Victrix* exploited every conceivable device and effect in order to highlight the ultimate and glorious triumph of the Christian faith. It marked the impressive climax of that golden sunset in which Latin, the language of ancient Rome, the Catholic church and Renaissance humanism, for the last time gave voice to the concerns of all and was understood by most. Those who could not understand were amply compensated by an awe-inspiring deployment of every facet of baroque stagecraft: allegorical interludes, dances, marine battles, choruses, portents and omens, sacrifices and pagan rituals, heraldic emblems, Christian symbols and classical allusions, all merged with contemporary preoccupations into a vast and cosmic drama.

Its impact on ear and eye was irresistible. Constantine's victory over his pagan rival Maxentius at the Battle of the Milvian Bridge in AD 312 was its subject: 'Caesar in isto signo vinces!' — 'O Caesar, in this sign shalt thou conquer!', the celestial choir proclaims as the spectacle opens to show us the struggle here below between the rival emperors and their evil or altruistic counsellors, while over their heads and ours Piety and Godlessness wage aerial battle in a baroque ceiling come alive with din and movement, colour and the cadences of Latin rhetoric. The virile vitality of Avancini's style was much praised; after all, it ideally suited this grandiose vindication of the Christian faith, the prime purpose underlying all Jesuit theatricals. And the implicit eulogy of his Holy Roman and Imperial Majesty was a gratifying confirmation to contemporaries that great traditions were still alive and that all was well with the world. Imagine the delighted awe, the holy hush which came over that vast audience as the Blessed Virgin Herself appeared, while angels lauded Leopold to the skies, proclaiming that in himself alone he united all the virtues of every prince to have ruled before him. To posterity the golden glory of it all seems tarnished: the theatrical conventions have vanished as has the language too, along with our readiness to believe in what was depicted and what it stood for. Yet its immediacy then was total.

The performance of *Pietas Victrix* in Vienna in 1659 was one of the outstanding cultural events of the baroque age: a transient moment when the relatively provincial literary and theatrical achievements of the Jesuit tradition in Counter-Reformation Europe attained a counterpart of their great churches. From their prototype, the forward-looking Gesù in Rome, mother church of the Society of Jesus and designed by Vignola in 1568, and its northern pendant, St Michael's in Munich (1583), these had carried the immediately recognizable Jesuit architectural image — an imposing façade with pilasters and sculptured embellishments, and a spacious interior designed for audibility and directing all attention on to the altar — all over the world, to Mexico and Goa, Peru and the Philippines, and thereby exerted incalculable influence on baroque religious architecture. But the influence of the Jesuits on the baroque was more far-reaching than that. Their theologians and thinkers, men like Molina and Bellarmin, Suárez and Gracián, moulded intellectual patterns at the highest level, while the *Spiritual Exercises* of St Ignatius Loyola affected the whole course of personal devotion and thus the evolution of baroque religious and mystical poetry. They had the private ear of most Catholic rulers; but it was also as educators of the general public that they did much to condition and shape the culture of the baroque. 'Puerilis institutio est renovatio mundi' was their claim, and their educational programme *Ratio et Institutio Studiorum*, drawn up in 1599, provided the basis for the great teaching establishments like that at Vienna, which arose by the score during this period. The education of the Catholic upper classes was predominantly in Jesuit hands; organized and standardized on a worldwide scale, it may account in large part for the cosmopolitan nature of the baroque, and for those typical ideals and responses which can be encountered in all the countries in the least affected by Jesuit zeal in the frontline of seventeenth-century religious and moral conflict. And not least in the Netherlands, whose seven northern provinces had won their long rebellion against Spain and achieved the recognition of their independence in the Treaty of Westphalia, which brought the Thirty Years War in Europe to a close in 1648.

The culture of this rapidly expanding and prosperous power had as its outstanding exponent a great writer singularly at odds with its dominant characteristics of Calvinist sobriety and commercial self-confidence. Born in Cologne of refugee Anabaptist parents who had been forced to flee from Rubens's home town of Antwerp in the Spanish Netherlands, Vondel established himself in Amsterdam, and for the remainder of his long life (1587-1679) was recognized by his more discerning contemporaries as the greatest handler of the Dutch language and more — as the voice of his country's conscience. An epic poem on the subject of Constantine the Great and the triumph of Christianity in imperial Rome, constructed on the model of Tasso's *Jerusalem Delivered*, was interrupted by the shock of his wife's death: Vondel turned to tragedy — to tragedy such as the baroque age dreamt of but seldom achieved with such imaginative power, such compelling force of language. What moved this Dutchman to go over to Rome? Nostalgia, no doubt, for those ancient times when Christian faith and the church were one, their authority uncontested: times before sectarian bigotry and party whim had yet begun to trivialize and debase the monumental grandeur of the Christian message. It was a perplexing experience for seventeenth-century Dutchmen to realize that their greatest poet was giving voice to ideals and traditions by no means always in keeping with the homely realism of many of the Dutch painters. Yet Vondel is a great painter too: a baroque painter in words. But not for him those faithful pictures of the tranquil existence which was more usually the lot of his fellow mortals than was a life of pomp, of tragic suffering or of world-stirring actions: he turned his eye from village weddings, merchant ships becalmed, hanging game and cattle grazing, to loftier visions of heroic warriors, prophets and cloud-borne angels, but with just as much respect for the precious quality of truthfulness that emanates from the paintings of Ruisdael or Vermeer, Hals or Rembrandt.

The first great work to reveal the full nature of the spiritual and artistic decision he was making appeared in 1639: *Maeghden* ('The Maidens'), a grandiosely tragic survey of the legendary martyrdom of St Ursula and her 11,000 virgin companions in Vondel's beloved Cologne, 'faithful daughter of the Roman Church', as they were returning down the Rhine from a pilgrimage to Rome only to fall into the godless hands of the Hun Attila, the scourge of God. The subject seems impossible, at least for a tragic play: yet Vondel brings off the impossible, sure hallmark of a truly baroque achievement. The classical, Sophoclean devices of narration and dialogue are combined in such as way as to produce an effect at once visual and intellectual: the dramatist shows in words what cannot be told in action or understood in images alone: the martyrdom of 11,000 virgins and, underlying it, the fundamental clash between Christian conviction and heathen ruthlessness. And always the stress is on the showing, be it visionary or demonstrative, cerebral or appealing to the senses; true, that is, to the visual notion of 'showing' implicit in the Dutch term for theatre, which is *Schouwburg* — Amsterdam's civic theatre, the envy of Northern Europe, had first opened its doors in 1637/8 — true also to the demonstrative gesture, the deictic manner, which was so much part of the baroque stance. Thus here, in the first act, Attila's trusted commander Julian describes Ursula's astonishing water-borne approach towards her future killer, himself soon to become infatuated by his captive's unattainable and fundamentally incomprehensible charms. Subtly the description at once attracts and warns: it is an image of virginal purity moving militant and confident into the centre of attention, and pictorially evoked in bold yet tender whites and reds, the colouring dominant throughout this whole great painting in words:

> She stood — and what a proud, defiant stance! —
> On the first ship, her banner in her hand,
> A crown of diamonds and rubied roses on her:
> But, lovelier still, those blooming on her face,
> Most beautiful when glowing with the flush
> Which noblest blood brought welling to each cheek.
> Upon her bosom glowed and played the arms
> Of a gold cross, all set with choice blue sapphires:
> Luxuriant breezes too played now and then,
> Filling the sail or rippling the flag
> Tied to her standard cross, in which she trusted.
> These were her armoury, and all her spears:

Her eye, a sharper spear, transfixed my heart.
Her purple garment with its sleeves of white
Was now and then raised by the tender winds.
The lily and the rose in golden thread
Were kindled into brightness by the sun
Which set for envy. . .

The stance, the baroque imagery of rose and lily, spear and sun, the wind and water and the tangible insignia of faith, all borne upon an undercurrent of erotic admiration: the colour, movement, visual force and symbolic effect of this one speech all convey the nature of this dramatic exaltation of spiritual values apprehended in sensual terms. This Christian Amazon, this chaste champion of Christ, proves herself to be more than an equal for the scourge of God. His threats, his might, his passion are in vain, for they all come up against the immutable defiance of her complete confidence in a greater vision: Ursula longs to mingle the purple with the white, and don the blood-red livery of the martyr. 'Zo triomfeert men overwonnen' — thus in defeat she triumphs over the heathen despot whose own downfall is imminent. As the burgomaster, archbishop and citizens of Cologne watch aghast from the ramparts of their besieged city, the 11,001 innocents are massacred. And Vondel spares his audience no gory or affecting detail in a choral narration which balances crassest emotional and descriptive detail with coolest, most controlled form to complete perfection.

The real martyrs of the baroque age were priests and soldiers; the martyrs so often depicted in its literature and painting, however, were beautiful young women, and understandably so. This springs less perhaps from any deep psychological and erotic motivations than from its instinct for the allegorical dimension; its readiness, that is, to accept figures that are half-human, half-personification. This St Ursula, like the two St Catherines, represents in part the fair embodiment of Christian faith and piety: only her outward charms appeal to the barbarian Attila; the inner meaning she embodies he is blind to. And this propensity to embody, to represent, to show or set forth, is a dominant feature of the baroque. Princes and rulers subsumed in their persons and effigies countless virtues and qualities of good government, and lesser mortals were no less immune to the responsibilities and effects of the face they showed the world. But allegories are incomprehensible without a context,

embodiments meaningless if not incorporated in a scene or framework familiar to the beholder. And this is what design and
composition provided. Architects, painters, writers, all are intent
on achieving the same final effect: grouping, symmetry, contrast,
recurring images, allusions are all means of attaining it. That is why
it is indeed possible to describe Vondel's Ursula in terms of the
other arts — to see it as a grandiose altarpiece, the product of
painting, sculpture and architecture combined. The red of robe and
blood and roses, the chaste whiteness of virginity, with suggestions
of gold in diadem, crucifix and sunlight: these are soon transformed by the visual imagination into porphyry and marble, with
the gleam of gilt; the ornamental setting which encloses a spiritual
picture at once static and convulsed with movement. St Ursula
stands unmovable in her conviction, unmoved by raging threats
and amorous entreaties, while in the background the Rhine flows in
majestic silver spate past the walls and pinnacles of Cologne, a holy
city then, and now in the seventeenth century the headquarters of
the Jesuits' campaigns to reconquer Protestant Europe for the
Roman church.

5

Turks, Moors & mariners

The Turks laid siege to Vienna in 1683. In the following year the
Moroccan seaport of Tangier, which had come to Britain with
Bombay as part of the dowry of Charles II's Portuguese queen, was
once again lost to the Moors. The political importance of these two
events, like the commercial, may be relative; but between them they
do in their different ways suggest why it was that the Islamic world
had its part to play in shaping and colouring the culture of the
baroque in Europe.

The middle years of the seventeenth century were ones of
political and military recovery in the Ottoman Empire, and the
Turkish menace, which had already provided a disturbing counterpoint to the achievements of the Renaissance period in Germany
and Eastern Europe especially, was growing so ominous that in
retrospect one can only marvel at the indifference which was
displayed towards it. By the 1670s Turkish frontiers in Europe were
more extensive than ever before. But baroque culture is not only
characterized by a fondness for sharp contrasts but also by the
ability to overlook or even to court dangers of which it was well
aware. Just as death lurked in Arcadia, the armed presence of the
Turk massing outside the gates of Europe was very much an
accepted part of the European scene. Like some reincarnation of the
Byzantine Empire which the Turks had destroyed 200 years before,
the Christian courts and governments of the West were prone to
pass their days in alternating displays of luxury and pleasure-seeking

and violent outbursts of religious fervour, and to concentrate their official attention on the niceties of pedigree and etiquette, with only occasional forays against the common enemy without. And of none was this more true than of the Holy Roman Empire. To the more erudite — and they were many among the relatively small section of society which produced culture and consumed it — the presence of oriental foes along the imperial borders suggested gratifying analogies with the Greece and Rome of Alexander the Great and Mithridates, the Carthaginians and Persians. In this respect the 'Asia Minor' of so many of the French plays of the period was not quite as remote and insubstantial as it now seems. However, a new dimension had been added to what might seem but a repetition of an earlier historical situation, and this was that Europe seldom felt so Christian as when its thoughts turned to the Turkish menace. Around the infidel figures conjured up by its imagination there tended to gather many of the vices and short-comings of which it was uneasily conscious in itself, and which it could more easily detect and deplore when they were sharply set off against epitomes of Christian virtue. Sometimes an oriental setting or an Islamic figure would even be invested with unsuspected qualities which then, by implication, could be used to show up the disappointing standards of conduct and morality at home.

In the realms of poetry and the attendant arts of illustrative painting and dramatic music, great impetus had been given to these lines of thought by *Jerusalem Delivered*. This universally admired epic had occupied the Italian poet Tasso (1544-95) during his finest years, and it captured the imagination of his fellow countrymen when it first appeared in 1581. Soon references to it spread far and wide in Europe as men and women from an extraordinarily varied social spectrum discovered its delights; from Venetian gondolier to English parson, Catholics and Protestants found themselves united in their fondness for a work whose subject was nothing less than the encounter between East and West. Some savoured its poetic beauty in the original, for Italian was the most widely read language in Europe, and many others derived their pleasure from more or less reliable translations: *Godfrey of Bulloigne* (1601) by Edward Fairfax was the standard one in English, and Diederich von dem Werder's *Gottfried von Bulljon* (1626) its counterpart in German. Relevant in every way to its own age and for a century or more to come, Tasso's subject was very

much a Counter-Reformation dream brought to life by his passionate imagination and retold in a manner which possessed most of the
qualities and features then admired. And Tasso invested it with all
the heroic distance traditionally expected of an epic poem, and
made it more acceptable to readers in other European and non-
Catholic countries by setting it back in the medieval days of the
First Crusade when the forces of united Christendom, led by
Godfrey of Bouillon, had recaptured the Holy City of Jerusalem.
All the old qualities of idealized romance and chivalry sprang to life
again, and their appeal especially to that new type of man, the
'cavalier' (they solaced Charles I in his confinement), shows that
there is a distant link between the ethos of the Middle Ages and the
values held by the baroque. But, in accordance with the new
conventions established by the Renaissance, Tasso submitted his
account of peerless knighthood and matchless devotion to the
rigorous disciplines of form and language. The Middle Ages and
the classical antiquity of Greece and Rome were synthesized, the
achievements of Homer and of Virgil fused with those of courtly
poem and chivalrous romance, and the whole quickened with
heroic passion and the spiritual fervour of the Counter-Reformation.
On a foundation as generously and ably laid as this, what wonder
that successive generations built! And so the *Gerusalemme liberata*
came to be one of the normative achievements of its age through its
intrinsic qualities and pivotal position in European culture. In due
course, as part of Italy's wider influence, it was to radiate out to almost every part of Europe. As a result, many of its characters and episodes became the inspiration of writers, painters and musicians and
thus play a part both direct and indirect in the formation of the new
culture: countless are the references, for instance, to the tragic loves
of the crusader Tancred and the warrior maid Clorinda in the art of
the baroque period, for here Tasso's world is acceptable even to those
who cannot share his ardent Catholic convictions, let alone to a great
Catholic musician such as Monteverdi. His extended dramatic duet *Il
combattimento di Tancredi e Clorinda* (1624) provides a passionately Italianate counterpart to Lully's ample and dignified lyric tragedy *Armide*, which in 1689 provided the French court with a large-
scale entertainment based on the final victory of the Christian hero
Rinaldo over the Saracen sorceress Armida. This episode, at once spiritual and erotic, proved to be one of the most captivating of all baroque
subjects; Rinaldo's captivity on Armida's enchanted island, where

> The quiet seas below lie safe and still,
> The green wood like a garland grows aloft,
> Sweet caves within, cool shades and waters shrill,
> Where lie the nymphs on moss and ivy still. . .

a setting which was an endless source of inspiration to painters and musicians, and to designers of parks, gardens and open-air festivities.

Enchanted islands, with their perfumed air and golden strands with pearls and corals strewn, became very much part of the imagination; islands where adventurous men, at least in fiction, can set foot in an earthly paradise.

> Oh happy men! that have the grace
> This bliss, this heaven, this paradise to see
> This is the place wherein you may assuage
> Your sorrows past, here is that joy and bliss
> That flourished in the antique golden age,
> Here needs no law, here none doth aught amiss:
> Put off those arms and fear not Mars his rage,
> Your sword, your shield, your helmet needless is;
>   Then consecrate them here to endless rest,
>   You shall love's champions be, and soldiers blest. . .

sings the 'naked wanton' to the doughty knights intent on rescuing Rinaldo from his amorous exile; for this island paradise is also one in which forces less benign may well be lurking to seduce them. The island theme is one that recurs throughout the period which runs from Shakespeare's late, perhaps even last play *The Tempest* (1611) to Defoe's *Life and Strange Surprising Adventures of Robinson Crusoe*, that grippingly realistic yet often moralizingly dated novel which, appearing in 1719, clearly marks the break then generally taking place everywhere in Europe between the baroque and a later, very different age. In Defoe's story the fictitious island is a very 'real' one in a way in which baroque islands never are. For the topography of their imaginative world is not one which reckons in yards and miles or goes by maps and charts: it has no truck with places realistically described. Colour it loved; but it had scant respect for 'local colour' in the modern sense. It delighted in detail, yet had no respect for 'scientifically' accurate documentation. Its ornate and carefully wrought descriptions were of places off the map and existing only through the force of words or the skill of draughtsmanship. But to no period in modern history have islands mattered more. From the moment when Columbus landed on San Salvador, mistaking it for an outpost of Japan, and planted the Saviour's banner in its sands to take possession of it in the name of Spain, the mercantile and naval expansion of Europe was closely associated with the quest for islands; after all, their discovery and capture promised enormous wealth and commercial monopoly of what were then the major trades, gold and spices. 'The winds breathed spikenard, myrrh, and balm around', and those same people who in Venice and in London delighted in Armida's island or Miranda's were at the same time intent on fighting the Turk for control of Rhodes and Cyprus, or to get the better of the Portuguese and Dutch in Ceylon and the Moluccas. Meanwhile, from the Spanish convents in the New World to the Jesuit missions in Japan, the interests of religion went hand in hand with those of war and trade, adding a spiritual dimension to European rivalries, just as they did to the strife between Crusader and Saracen in Tasso's epic. For on the economic front, as on the religious, baroque Europe was disunited. The Protestant powers of Britain and the Netherlands fought each other over the Indies, Spain dominated its rival Portugal, and Venice, once the unquestioned gateway to the East, began to sink into its long decline.

The Venice of 1600 was the opulent background for *Othello, The Moor of Venice* (1604), a tragedy played out on the island of Cyprus during the Venetian struggle against the 'general enemy Ottoman'. In his dramatization of sublimest passion undermined by envious duplicity, Shakespeare anticipated the tastes and preoccupations of the century, as its admiration for his play bears out. Othello himself, valiant, heroic, yet capable of the most tender devotion, has much in him of Tasso's epic heroes; yet within him, and brought to the surface by the villainous ploys of Iago and the effects of overheated passion, lurk those very dangers against which these epic heroes fought — the very hallmarks of their foe. For valiant Othello is a lascivious Moor, proud, jealous and easily inflamed to passion: a man in whom the zest for living outstrips the norm of humankind, a child of nature naïve in his responses yet presumptuous in the claims he makes upon himself and others. To the trumpet's sound the Moor sets foot on Cyprus to defend it — strange paradox — against the Turkish enemy: is not Othello an

enemy within the gates? 'O my fair enemy!' he greets the Italian
Desdemona, like Tancred his Ethiopian Clorinda,

> O my soul's joy!
> If after every tempest come such calms,
> May the winds blow till they have waken'd death!

The grandiloquent gallantry of the compliment, which aptly turns
real sea voyage and just-navigated storm into an erotic image or
conceit, brings to the play a breath of that new manner, Italianate
and ornate, which was to reappear with such panache in the brasher
yet often simpler words of Dryden's dramatic heroes. But in
Othello the winds of passion really waken death. The jealous
violence of the infidel Moor finally destroys his façade of Christian
self-control and chivalrous decorum as he strangles the chaste white
Desdemona in her bed—an outcome far removed from that which
baroque taste was to demand of its heroes even if they were Moors,
but entirely in keeping with what it expected of its Turkish villains.

This most formalized and passionate of Shakespeare's tragedies,
and the one which comes closest to seventeenth-century taste, takes
place, significantly, upon an island in those Mediterranean waters
where the forces of Christendom, supplied by Venice, Genoa and
Rome, had won the most decisive naval battle of the whole post-
Reformation period. It was one of the rare moments of European
glory in an era which thirsted for displays of martial valour: the
Christian victory which inspired Tasso to write his epic of a dream
crusade. And its victor, Don John of Austria, natural son of the
Emperor Charles V, coming straight from the defeat of the North
African Moors to crush the Turks, seemed to embody all the
qualities and virtues of his Habsburg ancestors, while at the same
time taking after his Spanish forebears Ferdinand and Isabella, who
had achieved that earlier turning point in Europe's fortunes when,
in 1492, they retook Granada, and put an end to Islamic power and
culture on Western European soil — a turning point which had
then seemed as momentous as the discovery of the New World in
that same year.

The New World and the Mediterranean — the appeal of both
these areas of geopolitical concern was felt well into the seventeenth
century, and by none more strongly than Dryden, a man whose flair
for topical issues makes him reflect, as no other Englishman does,
the interests, ideas and enthusiasms of contemporary Europe. In

1665 he brought his lively imagination to bear on the new London fashion for heroic tragedies, entertainments of a lavish and extrovertly elegant kind on the model of the French plays — such as those of Thomas Corneille — which the Stuart court had come to admire during its Cromwellian exile, and which the growing influence of France now made all the more appealing. He opened his campaign to naturalize a truly baroque form of stage entertainment with *The Indian Queen*, extravagantly set in the Mexico and Peru of Aztecs and Incas before the Spanish conquest. Whatever the immediate reasons for this unlikely choice, it does reflect something of the English interest in transatlantic matters. Mrs Aphra Behn, the well-known authoress, actually supplied a set of plumes for the Indian queen to borrow; they came from Surinam (Guyana) and were infinitely admired by persons of quality, which makes it clear that stage effects and fripperies had now become something that really mattered. Later she was herself to exploit her personal associations with exotic climes in that fine blend of realism and romance, her story of the noble savage Oroonoko, a negro king enslaved both to a European planter and to the charms of Imoinda, his beautiful fellow slave. As Mrs Behn's gallant savage meets his ignominious death at European hands, he displays all the mutinous pride and greatness of soul that characterize those idealized baroque heroes who generally inhabit worlds more civilized and˙ artificial than seventeenth-century Surinam.

Dryden continued in his pre-Columbian vein with his next play, *The Indian Emperor*, which presents the headlong encounter between that unknown world and the new Europe represented by Spanish Cortez. Then, after *Tyrannic Love* and a brief but triumphant foray into the European world of baroque martyrdom, the time was ripe for England's most resounding Moorish venture, *The Conquest of Granada* (in two parts, 1670-1). Against the turbulent background of conflict and intrigue, betrayal and selfless valour, its hero Almanzor pursues his love for Almahide with such astounding dash and a passion so exalted that he touches on the extremest bounds of what is credible:

> Vast is his courage, boundless is his mind,
> High as a storm and humorous as wind.
> Honour's the only idol of his eyes. . .

And so on. Yet the preposterous grandiloquence of these idealized figures and their heroic posturing cannot conceal the fact that Dryden's imaginary Moorish Granada is a state torn, like any other, by conflicting politics, party interests and factions, each pursuing its own ends and representing an enemy within more insidiously potent than the attacking forces of self-righteous Christendom. The proud pursuit of love and honour and the deceitful lust for power and wealth are both shown to be disruptive; both tend to lead to a confusion of man's true aims. Illusion, wishful thinking and self-indulgence are inextricably caught up with the nobler impuses of pride and self-esteem which signal out a hero. Almahide chides Almanzor for his piratical behaviour, and the analogy is appropriate, for the piracy on the Barbary coast of Algeria and Morocco was well known as a major risk run by all Mediterranean seafarers. But this hint of proud loneliness and buccaneering self-assertion suits a hero who can also in less hectic mood give voice to notions of a kind which go right to the heart of the baroque age's most serious concerns:

> O Heaven, how dark a riddle's thy decree,
> Which bounds our wills, yet seems to leave them free:
> Since thy foreknowledge cannot be in vain,
> Our choice must be what thou didst first ordain.

Such words sound like a summary of the most obsessive worries of Dryden's contemporaries, worries which underlie its most deeply considered and lasting achievements, and which also largely prompted the acrimonious debates and differences which raged in many places and in different forms, and which were such a characteristic manifestation of the intellectual climate. The Jesuits and Jansenists in France are one example, arguing out the problems of free will and the operation of divine grace; or the Arminians and Gomarists in Holland, in similar disagreement on similar questions, though in this case seen through reformed and Calvinistic eyes. But then Almanzor goes on, and with his author's innate command of the apt image transcends the theological commonplaces of those lines with:

> Then, like a captive on an isle confin'd,
> Man walks at large, a prisoner of the mind;
> Wills all his crimes, while Heaven the indictment draws,
> And, pleading guilty, justifies the laws.

The theology may be orthodox enough; but what an abyss opens up! For these are sentiments whose resonances reach out far and wide, to haunt the reader of a later period to whom the ideas themselves may seem remote, but certainly not the image. Such are the pleasures waiting for anyone prepared to look at baroque works on their merits.

While Dutch clergymen of austere mien and awesome learning debated weighty topics of this kind with the ponderous passion of their calling, their parishioners were often setting sail in solid merchantment to cross the vastness of the seventeenth-century oceans in search of trade and to the greater glory and prosperity of the Dutch East India Company. Established in 1602, it soon became the basis of the swift expansion of the century's major European maritime trading nation: by 1660 more than 15,000 of the 26,000 ships sailing the European seas were said to be flying the Dutch ensign, and Amsterdam had become the undisputed centre not just of shipping, but of modern banking and insurance too. A curious amalgam that nation was, and just as characteristic a creation of its age as the France of Louis XIV or the England of the two Charleses and the Lord Protector. Efficient yet ill organized; strict, yet easy-going to a high degree, it reconciled within the confines of one society divergent claims and contradictory aspirations, thus deserving its reputation as a model of government, albeit no utopia. Though Protestant, its sober reformed religion did not preclude a remarkable degree of tolerance, allowing ideas to circulate with unusual freedom. It sheltered the victims of persecution, such as communities of pious and successful Jews expelled from Spain and Portugal, among their number Baruch Spinoza (1632-77), perhaps the major abstract thinker of the baroque age. In God or nature Spinoza saw the ultimate unity of all things, and thus regarded good and evil as relative to the individual interests of men. In the absolute state such conventional moral distinctions are transcended, for in reality everything that is and all that happens is preordained and inevitable. Happy the man who can brace himself to such insights into reality! Happy the man who can accept the fact that everything must be as perforce it is in this the only possible world, and thus appreciate the bounds and limits of his natural state! Consistent with himself and with this baffling world he will be free to renounce impossible illusions in an austere display of moral strength and nobility of mind. To Spinoza as a baroque thinker such realism must govern states as well as men: both necessarily live in a 'state of nature' with each other, striving continually to extend their influence and power, and each concludes or breaks alliances as suits their interests or serves their self-preservation. Such views, expressed in the *Theological-Political Treatise* of 1670 and in the *Ethics* published on his death, reflect ideas and take up lines of thought already suggested or advanced by Hobbes, Descartes, and the many others who contributed to the intellectual structure of the age and formulated versions of it in their various countries, languages and traditions. An ideology emerged soon in evidence all over Europe, and well suited to transcend frontiers and unite thinking men. It was the achievement of a philosopher like Spinoza to give lasting intellectual shape and substance to the attitudes and conduct which surrounded him. Between his ideal man and Dryden's heroes there is much in common; and in the causes and conduct of the various wars which gave expression to Anglo-Dutch rivalry at sea and formed the background for those Dryden plays, Spinoza's view of human motivation and international politics was borne out.

The right of nations to control the seas had been examined by Grotius, the great Dutch lawyer who, in his *Mare liberum* of 1609, had ruled that, like the firmament, the oceans of this earth are open to one and all. The expansive right and freedom thus expressed reflect the sense of opportunity which was being generated by the expansion of merchant shipping and by new discoveries overseas. One of the implications of this new sense of space was the conception of this world as a globe enclosing untold riches awaiting the courageous seeker ready to explore it to the full. Opportunism and glorious enterprise: there was something of both about it, as Vondel realized when in 1623 he wrote his grandiose poem *In Praise of Navigation* (*Het lof der zeevaart*). Its copious lines convey the self-confidence, the sense of promise and proud achievement which this expansion fostered: lines in which apposite mythological allusions are jostled by the jargon of deck and quayside — the local and the timeless interfused in the broad sweep of the poet's imagination, like those Dutch canvases of the period, with merchantmen becalmed or cutting the water, their bulging sails filled with a favourable wind, their pennants rippling, the sunlight glinting on their gold-encrusted poops.

                    It seems as if they're building
Church towers out to sea, from which you may perchance
Survey the world as from some pinnacle:
No, no, those are not masts or fighting-tops; they're chains
To venture further and make Olympus fast!

Such are the poet's sentiments as he watches the display of
Holland's seaborne strength launched on a boundless ocean. He
speaks almost as if he were an Amsterdam merchant or at least
owned shares in the East India Company:

              At last to see my ship on even keel,
              Riding at anchor in the stream:
              This surely is a dream!

This proud wonderment soon turns into a glowing declaration of
love, a panegyric of truly baroque dimensions, but addressed not to
some creature of the erotic poet's imagination; the loved one here is
that very real object of a Dutchman's passion — a ship, supreme
achievement of that seventeenth-century technology which even
drew Czar Peter the Great of Russia to the shipyards of the
Netherlands:

              O godlike vessel! you allure my senses.
              A mirthful mermaid or a watery bridge,
              You hold King Neptune captive in your golden hair
              As he espies the jewels hanging in your ear;
              You look like Venus on her course for Cyprus
              Across the living marble of the sea. . .
              Great Proteus! what wonder mortal man
              Disdains the plough and longs for the sea air!
              And this despite the fact he knows full well
              The ship will heave and plunge deaf to the arts
              Of sea-craft, astrolabe and wheel, storm-tossed
              And at the mercy of a tempest raging
              Like inflamed Janissaries deaf to a Sultan's will.

Thus the sea imagery of the erotic poet and all the apparatus of
mythology blend with rich descriptive detail and the buoyancy
borne of economic expansion to sing the praises of nothing more
nor less than maritime achievement. And into the fabric of his
eulogy the poet incorporates, because they are so apt, those

references to Cyprus and to Turkey. For in their way they too are
quite at home in this vast poem, this monument, as he calls it, built
in words to show forth the majesty of the world's eighth wonder,
before which even the black-skinned Moors will fall upon their
knees, provided always it preserve itself from greed and violence
and remember that economics, too, are entirely subject to the
immutable laws of nature and of providence.

Vondel's *Lof der zeevaart* is one of the great poems of baroque
Europe. And it is one which, thanks to its wide frame of references,
conveys both a panorama and the specific feel of life in those days,
its challenges and its main assumptions. Its exalted spaciousness
and sense of order, its pace, the ebb and flow of images succeeding
each other in fluid sequences which satisfy the mind because they
build up meaning — significant details highlighted, but never at
the expense of overall design and fuller pattern — these are facets
of its quality. But in the last resort it is the tone of voice with which
the poet proclaims the mastery of nature over man and of
Dutchmen over nature that invests his eulogy with something of
the quality one associates with the Dutch painters of marine
subjects: painters such as Aelbert Cuyp (1620-90), Jan van de
Cappelle (*c.* 1624-79) and Willem van de Velde the younger (1633-
1704), in whose many canvases the bold spirit of the Dutch navy
and merchant fleet is seen in terms of teeming craft, of pennants,
masts and rigging, against a background of enormous sky. Pictorially rich and full of minute detail, their bustling vitality caught for
ever in spontaneously ordered repose, such paintings, like Vondel's
poem, cause space to open up and show forth a deeper figurative
meaning. Dutch maritime prosperity becomes a visual and contemporary emblem of human life itself.

Thither the wealth of all the world did flow. Yet despite a
commanding commercial position and maritime supremacy
throughout the finest years of the baroque period, the United
Provinces never produced that epic which would have given lasting
shape and immortality to their achievements in the manner most
esteemed by post-Renaissance taste. How different Portugal,
though sixty years' captivity, for such they called it, were to chain
her destinies to those of Spain from that dire day in 1578 when her
young and headstrong King Sebastian, thirsting for martial glory
and aspiring to be the champion of Christendom against the Moors,
had led his armies to disastrous defeat in North Africa. Sebastian

died upon the battlefield, and the aftermath of this eclipse saw his country lose her monopolies to the Netherlands, traditional enemies of Philip II of Spain who now ruled over his kingdom in default of other heirs. But however bad her treatment in the harsh world of seventeenth-century power politics, Portugal did have the consolation of an epic which expressed her sense of national destiny. *Os Lusíadas* appeared in 1571. It had been written by Luis Vaz da Camoens mainly in the oriental settings of Macao, Portugal's colony in China, and in Goa, the thriving Indian seaport and symbolic centre of Christian influence in the East, shrine of St Francis Xavier, its Apostle. This Jesuit missionary, like a new St Thomas or St Paul, was one of the most popular and outstanding embodiments of the ideals of conquering cross and Christian expansion; so is Camoens' poem. For it succeeds in creating an extraordinary blend of old and modern by juxtaposing an account of Vasco da Gama's voyage round the Cape of Good Hope to Calicut in India with retrospective digressions back to Portugal's own medieval past and championship of Christianity against the infidel, and with allusions to classical Rome and the deities of mythical Olympus. Virgil is seldom far away; but nor are the quays and hostelries of Lisbon, its yarn-spinning mariners and its great ships venturing forth in search of precious cargo, the gold and jewels and spices of India, China and Brazil.

For on the one hand *Os Lusíadas* is an epic poem which reflects the mentality and values of contemporary men — disdain and yet desire for fortune, stress on fortitude and Christian faith, buoyant heroism, self-assertion, and a deep awareness of human frailty and smallness too — yet on the other hand it also opens up for the first time a vision of that imaginative world which was to become the familiar domain of baroque Europe. Take, for example, the 'Palace of Neptune' in Canto VI, evocative of innumerable fountains and cascades which in seventeenth-century parks and gardens sought to fuse the cool curves and splashes of moving water with the static bulk of rough-hewn rock and stone:

> In the abstrusest Grottoes of the Deep,
> Where th'Ocean hides his head far under ground,
> There, whence to play their pranks the Billows creep,
> When (mocking the lowd Tempests) they resound,
> Neptune resides. There wanton Sea-Nymphs keep,

And other Gods That haunt the Seas profound,
Where arched Waves leave many Cities dry,
In which abides each watry Deity.

What Camoens expresses with such mastery in his poem is no doubt
what many mariners also thought and felt on baroque seas. Indeed
the figureheads on ships and the lore surrounding them are modern
reminders of the extent to which the mythology of seafare is a
product of a fusion of experience and art which took place then,
and which Camoens, the Portuguese adventurer-poet, captured
and embodied in his work.

This fusion, and his tendency to anticipate the artistic and poetic
climate of the seventeenth century, are particularly evident in the
celebrated episode of the 'Isle of Love', which occurs in Canto IX.
The stalwart sailors of Vasco da Gama's fleet catch sight of the Isle
of Love just as dawn is breaking. With its gleaming strand studded
with roseate shells, it is an imaginary extension of reality, of those
Indies which were then still being discovered; on it Venus,
protectress of the Portuguese, those new Argonauts or Trojans
embarked in Christian search for gold, has conjured up an earthly
paradise finer than mortals yet have found or even dreamed of:

In fine, an Inn of pleasure by the way
To bait and strengthen tyr'd Humanity,
To give her gallant Sea-men, not their Pay,
But the use here of fair Eternity.

This foretaste of paradise regained, the Lusitanian heroes savour to
the full. But the ocean's beautiful nymphs and the angelic painted
island (it could be painted on a baroque ceiling) are in fact no
more, the poet assures us, than symbols of the honours which make
our lives sublime:

The privileges of the Martial Man,
The Palm, the Lawrell'd Triumph, the rich spoile,
The admiration purchas't by the sword,
These are the joys this Island doth afford.

Helpfully, Camoens now goes on to explain a point which is of the
greatest relevance to our understanding of this vanished culture and
its modes of expression. Antiquity, he says, which loved illustrious
men, invented immortalities upon starry Olympus for those who

soared aloft borne on the wings of valorous actions done in the path of virtue. And it was fame, trumpeting such exploits, which gave them in this world of ours the strange names of immortal gods and demigods. Awaken then from your ignoble sleep, curb avarice and unworthy ambition and the black and detestable vice of tyranny. Vain honours are a gold that is worth nothing! Either in peace promote impartial laws, or clothe yourselves in burning armour against the law of hostile Saracens! Again, the climax of this vision of heroism and its just rewards returns to the pervasive theme of Islamic menace. It runs all through the poem, just as it permeated the real and imaginary worlds of which it is such an extraordinarily true and memorable expression.

Camoens sees the Islamic menace as a pagan foil to Christian Portugal, and as a warning. With a cultural daring almost unparalleled in the serious art of the time, he equates it with Bacchus, mythological conqueror of India, and god of disorder and intoxication. This ancient deity steps out of his conventional role and comes to life again in the new world, jealous that the Christians' oriental exploits may eclipse his own. The equation is a telling one, for it was indeed the 'Dionysian' dangers of the Moslem world which tended to be most stressed by baroque Europe. Immoral lusts and craven sensuality, these were the un-Christian vices most readily associated with the lascivious Moors and Turks.

Portugal's national epic and Dryden's heroic plays, especially those on 'Indian' or 'Moroccan' subjects, have qualities in common, and many a passage of the 1571 poem could easily be recast in the form and rhythm of Dryden's heroic couplets. In fact the translation made of it by the English cavalier Sir Richard Fanshawe during his enforced seclusion after the royalist defeat at Worcester, and published in 1655, shared with his English version of *Il Pastor Fido* linguistic and stylistic qualities which did much to acclimatize the baroque manner in England and thus to prepare the way for the taste of the Restoration; Fanshawe himself went on to help negotiate King Charles's Portuguese marriage and dowry, and spent his last years as British ambassador to Lisbon and Madrid. What of course the English heroic dramas lack is the purpose and cohesion given by a sense of national destiny. In this sense *Os Lusíadas* has a closer affinity with other aspects of Dryden's output and the English literature of his age. Da Gama is a national 'worthy' like King Arthur. But the attempts of Dryden (in his

operatic venture with Purcell in 1691) and especially of Sir Richard
Blackmore (*King Arthur*, an epic poem, 1697) to create a sense of
epic purpose and contemporary relevance around the nebulous
figure of that legendary British monarch did not succeed. And this
was due in part no doubt to the fact that Arthur's traditional
enemies carried far less topical conviction than the Moors and
Saracens against whom Tasso's and Camoens' heroes have to fight;
even the offstage Moors routed by Don Rodrigue in Corneille's *Le
Cid* (1636) are more graphically present thanks to the hero's
splendidly exciting Act IV narration. None the less, affinities of
mood and manner do suggest a deeper motivation underlying
Dryden's purpose in devising the concept of heroic drama in order
to entertain the worldly-wise audiences of Restoration London.
'That kind of poesy, which excites to virtue the greatest men, is of
the greatest use to human kind,' he writes in his Dedication of *The
Conquest of Granada* to the Duke of York, recent victor over the
Dutch at sea, and he then goes on to say, 'I have formed a hero, I
confess, not absolutely perfect, but of an excessive and over-boiling
courage; but Homer and Tasso are my precedents.'

Dryden tried hard to argue that 'an heroic play ought to be an
imitation, in little, of an heroic poem; and, consequently, that love
and valour ought to be the subject of it.' Where he did capture the
buoyant confidence of the Portuguese epic and for that matter the
sense of boundless achievement that distinguishes Vondel's epic
eulogy of maritime adventure, is in the closing stanzas of his
'historical poem' *Annus Mirabilis*, the 'Year of Wonders', 1666.
For here he was intent, as he explained, on celebrating the most
heroic subject any poet could devise — the victories and vicissitudes
of Britain by means of 'lively and apt description, dress'd in such
colours of speech that it sets before your eyes the absent object, as
perfectly and more delightfully then nature'. With Camoens, Tasso
and Vondel, Dryden here shares a baroque ability to recast the
heroic sense of destiny they each admired in Virgil in such a way
that the derived and generalized elements merge with the specific
and create an effect which is proud and confident, and which
succeeds in ordering a wide-ranging framework of references into
rhyme and rhythm:

> The *British* Ocean shall such triumphs boast,
>   That those who now disdain our Trade to share,

Shall rob like Pyrats on our wealthy Coast. . .

Thus to the Eastern wealth through storms we go;
But now, the Cape once doubled, fear no more:
A constant Trade-wind will securely blow,
And gently lay us on the Spicy shore.

The theme and flavour of *The Lusiads* and of *In Praise of Navigation* are in miniature conveyed in the final flourish of that stanza.

It is no wonder that this age of maritime adventure, with its admiration for heroic action, should in the courtly setting of its theatres have championed the lawless liberty of its 'Moorish' heroes who, with Almanzor, can boast:

But know, that I alone am King of me!
I am as free as nature first made man,
Ere the base laws of servitude began,
When wild in woods the noble savage ran.

The self-inflated lines with which Almanzor introduces himself in the first act of *The Conquest of Granada* express an outlook shared more or less emphatically by many lesser mortals who were the product or at least a byproduct of baroque culture in its broadest sense. It was an age of piracy. On the high seas men who had never heard the names of the great poets were acting out in cold blood that heroic love of self displayed by the grandiloquent rebels of the baroque imagination, with their disdain for public order and Christian virtue, and their pagan lust for love and gold and glory. Though Europeans, these buccaneers were the heirs of the Moorish corsairs of Tunis and Algiers who in the sixteenth century had infested the chief sea-trading routes of Europe, plundering ships with pitiless violence in revenge for their expulsion by Spain and in retribution for the Christian reconquest of Moorish Granada. The ominous presence of pirates in every ocean of the world, and the constant threat they presented to orderly imperial and religious expansion, was a stark reminder of the savage forces which, like Camoens' Bacchus, were felt to be at work ambushing Christian virtue and undermining the values of the West. The corsairs of the North African coast owed nominal allegiance to the Sultan of Turkey, the 'Grand Signior' as the Venetians called him, and in 1660 the Turkish Empire was at a zenith. The ambitious and gifted

Grand Viziers of the Kupruli family governed its fortunes, not its ineffective Sultans, and its expansion began to reach proportions which seriously disturbed both governments and the common people in many parts of Europe. An army of immense size was on the move; as the clouds gathered, the states of Christendom for a while almost overcame their differences. France broke her long-standing alliance with the Sultan, and her fleet bombarded Tunis, while in Central Europe the Christian armies, with the blessings of the Pope and Emperor Leopold and the assistance of Venetian men and money, inflicted on the unholy might of Turkey the resounding victory of St Gotthard an der Raab in 1664. For baroque Europe a turning point had been reached.

In the 1660s, the high-baroque decade in Europe, the Turkish menace was very much the centre of concern. Naturally the maritime nations of the West tended to see the conflict mainly in terms of sea-fights against Turkish outposts and allies on the African coast, and to reflect this view in their cultural response to it. But in the Central European states which formed the Holy Roman Empire the Moors of Restoration London and Portuguese poetry were peripheral indeed compared with the Turks themselves, while in France a subtly different slant was given to the situation as a result of a traditional pro-Turkish policy — part of Louis XIV's grand design to outdo his Habsburg rivals in Madrid and Vienna, and achieve French pride of place on sea and land. What in most other parts of Europe was a threatening embodiment of wantonness and lust, was prone in France to wear the more attractive appearance of that 'Turkish' fashion ridiculed in Molière's comedy *Le Bourgeois Gentilhomme* (1670) or made the exotic setting for the passions and tensions of Racine's harem tragedy *Bajazet* (1672). In her attitude to Turkey and what it stood for, France proved yet again to be something of an anomaly in baroque Europe. Very different was the view of Turkey held in those parts of Europe living closer to the menace of the rising crescent. In the Adriatic city-state of Ragusa (or Dubrovnik) on the Dalmatian coast, where Venetian influences merged with a tradition of proud Slav independence, the Turkish threat and Moslem—Christian conflict became the theme of a full-scale epic in the manner of *Jerusalem Delivered*, and equipped with all the network of digressions and displays of love and valour expected of a work cast in heroic mould. *Osman* by the Croatian poet Ivan Gundulić (1589-1638) narrates the rise, triumph

and bloody fall of Sultan Osman II, defeated by the Catholic might
of the Slav kingdom of Poland and done to death by his own
mutinous Janissaries in·1622. Of course this work is scarcely known
abroad; but it is a reminder that minor nations, too, shared
Europe's baroque ethos and its culture, and reaped their own
rewards in art and music. Their writers also gave expression to its
major themes with poems and plays which sought with more or less
conviction and distinction to adapt their respective languages to the
enormous demands of an essentially cosmopolitan phenomenon
more associated with the major powers. Few of the exponents of
Europe's minor languages achieved anything like Gundulić's
success.

The core of this Croatian conception of the Turkish theme lies in
the murder of the Sultan, a clear retribution for his evil and
impious deeds, and providentially ordained to help the Christians
without staining their hands in royal blood. The imperial might of
Turkey, which projects such dire menace, is in fact shown to be
corrupt within and to contain sufficient un-Christian vices to bring
about its own destruction. Europe, watching delighted and aghast
at contemporary events taking place in Turkey, was more than once
to see enacted there a sequence such as unfolded in *Osman*. In
1648, the year in which the Thirty Years War came to an end, and
with it those German internecine conflicts that so disfigured a
disunited Europe — the year also in which King Charles of England
was put on trial by his own parliament — a bloody conspiracy took
place in far-off Istambul. Ibrahim I, a dissolute and effete ruler
entirely at the mercy of his harem, was done to death by his own
family and soldiers. Insurrection flared up throughout the Turkish
Empire; disorder and anarchy followed in a paroxysm of wanton
lust and ruthless self-assertion. Here surely was a subject fit and
ready-made for baroque treatment.

Degenerate, ruthless and a showcase of all vices, such was the
Turkey depicted by Lohenstein in his last play, *Ibrahim Sultan*,
composed in honour of the Emperor Leopold's second marriage to
Claudia Felicitas, an Austrian archduchess, in 1673. Against the
Habsburg background of a matrimonial union between a lion's
regal strength and the pacific charms of sweet felicity, a dramatization of Turkish vice and Islamic menace seemed to contemporary
taste to be a choice of subject apt to the occasion and full of
promise. In symbolic as well as in political terms the play sets forth,

as its author puts it in his Dedication to the Emperor, the 'presently discernible eclipse of the Ottoman crescent moon', so as to show by an implied contrast the brilliant supremacy of the Sun of Austria, and that 'without lust there can be no love, nor rose without a thorn, no diamond without a flaw, nor gold without copper'. In other words we are, here, in a world of antitheses sharply caught and held in tense yet logical juxtaposition; an imaginative and symbolic world reflecting a concern for the issues of the day and their universal implications so vital and immediate that, beside it, the 'Turkish' ambience of Racine's *Bajazet*, produced one year before, seems artificial and remote. That delicate refinement of passion and of its linguistic expression, which is such a notable feature of Racine's tragedy, is not to be found in this, its German counterpart. Lohenstein's Turkey is as brash and discordant as the 'Turkish sound' which was then beginning to set an exotic fashion in Western music, and exerting a far-reaching influence on the evolution of the military band. The action of the play opens as the lust-crazed Sultan breaks open the door to a private chamber in an attempted rape. Later it will turn on the brutal seduction of Ambre, the innocent daughter of the Mufti or Islamic high-priest of Istambul, an act carried out while in the foreground antiphonal choruses of bathing wives, concubines and virgins sing the rival praises of voluptuous pleasure and chaste modesty. But this outrageous sacrilege will in its turn provoke its just revenge: the Sultan's violent overthrow, abdication and final degrading ritual strangulation by four of his own mutes.

Within its framework of allegorical prologue (in which the Bosphorus, aghast at Ibrahim's misdeeds, wells up in Leopold's more fortunate Vienna to spout timely compliments on the Emperor's marriage) and concluding masque (in which the allegorical figures of Claudia, doorkeeper of the Almighty, and Felicitas, embodiment of chastity and lust reconciled within the blissful bonds of holy matrimony, confront the shades of Ibrahim and Ambre to sing the praise of Habsburg), this feverish Turkish drama can unfold, sure in the knowledge that it will be seen in context and appreciated as part of a wider and more meaningful political, moral and aesthetic whole. Its atmosphere of concealed menace and claustrophobic tension, torrid lust and sexual decadence, cogently conveys exactly what Lohenstein's Turkey stood for: the incarnation of slavery in both the physical and psychological sense. And he can allow this ugly and antagonistic world to rise up before its spectators because it is so evident that his method of dual presentation parallels the relationship between stage play and theatrical setting or between allegorical painting and supporting architectural structure. Both elements are essential to the total vision and its effect. This is the quality that finally identifies and confirms Lohenstein's last play as a supreme baroque achievement.

Understandably enough, this product and reflection of the values of the 1670s was to arouse repugnance in the Age of Reason and disgust in that of Victorian prudery. Its thematic structure, like the purpose underlying its composition, was too immediately associated with the burning issues of the day; and its exotic quality was made still more alien by the uncompromisingly florid manner of Lohenstein's presentation. For every line on every page is heavily encrusted with the verbal equivalents of baroque ornament, and every metaphor and idea is sparked off, sustained and brought to a conclusion by what are in effect the poetic counterparts of those recurrent motifs which are such characteristic components of baroque design. Prominent among them are the proliferating references to fire and flames, to gold and jewellery, to sun and stars; to oriental motifs like pearls, roses, incense and spices; their highly wrought filigree controlled and dominated by an obsessive pattern of allusions to imperial purple and scarlet blood. In this ornate and tense counterfeit of the Turkish world it is not for nothing that certain rhymes in the German language are exploited to the full: *Blut* and *Glut* (blood and heat), *Lust* and *Brust* (pleasure and breast), *Zierde* and *Begierde* (jewel and desire) — for, like his exact contemporary Dryden, Lohenstein was convinced that rhyme was the 'noblest kind of modern verse', and that it enhanced sense rather than detracting from it.

In itself, this unheroic Turkish drama, with its emphasis on violence, intrigue and lust conveyed in commensurably ornate and coloured language, might not perhaps seem entirely to justify the claim that it epitomizes the attitudes of its age. Admittedly, many of them are already fully present in the issues raised and in the treatment they are given. But it is above all the relationship between the action itself and its formal setting in the framework provided by the prologue, masque-like interludes and allegorical conclusion that most compellingly expresses that characteristic interpenetration of formalized symbolism and reality which was

such an all-pervasive feature of the time. It was this quality that
enabled Lohenstein's *Ibrahim Sultan* to capture the very feel and
ethos of that struggle which, throughout the seventeenth century,
was being sporadically waged in central Europe between the
so-called Christian culture of the West and its traditional Oriental
enemy. For the Turks depicted in that play represented both the
hereditary foe of Christendom and a brutal antithesis or necessary
foil to the brilliant-ornate-pious but often distressingly disreput-
able civilization which created the splendours of the Belvedere
Palace in Vienna, built by the imperial architect Lucas von
Hildebrandt in 1721 for Prince Eugene, conqueror of the Turks, or
the Karlskirche, which was being erected at about the same time
there by Fischer von Erlach to symbolize not just the fusion of
pagan and Christian traditions in the Holy Roman Empire, but also
its universal destiny as represented by the twin columns of Constancy and Fortitude, those Roman pillars of Hercules which, on
either side of its portico, stand for the twin nations of Germany and
Spain, and point to wider action overseas.

A craven and licentious Sultan could provide a telling image of
evil in the Europe of the later seventeenth century, when the
spectre of Turkish depravity and cruelty exerted a widespread fear
and fascination. But it is significant that something of this same
atmosphere was evoked, at the height of his career, by Lohenstein's
contemporary Milton when intent on painting the infernal splendours of Pandemonium, the high capital of Satan and his peers.
Book II of *Paradise Lost* opens with a grandiose vision which in a
few lines calls into question so much of what the baroque age in
Europe most admired and valued:

> High on a throne of royal state, which far
> Outshone the wealth of Ormus and of Ind,
> Or where the gorgeous East with richest hand
> Showers on her kings barbaric pearl and gold,
> Satan exalted sat...
>   insatiate to pursue
> Vain war with Heaven.

Thus with a hyperbole that audaciously evokes all that seventeenth-
century seafarers and treasure-seekers were dreaming of and lusting
after, Milton invokes the Islamic image to reinforce and lend added
colour to a theme even loftier than that of Tasso's *Jerusalem*

Delivered: not just the reconquest of the Promised Land, but man's first disobedience and the loss of Eden.

6
Kings

'La face du théâtre change.' With these words Louis XIV announced his decision to assume personal power on the death of Cardinal Mazarin in 1661. The phrase has an authentic ring: this was indeed a major change of political direction as seen by a young monarch passionately fond of ballets, masques and operas and fully aware of the part he was to play. Not only do his words reflect a way of thinking prevalent at the time; they also suggest that those who, like the royal French actor, were at the centre of events knew exactly how much depended on a right choice of setting. The scene change he was referring to was becoming increasingly evident in many parts of Europe, and it was being reflected in art and literature. The entry of Louis le Dieudonné — the God-given — into his rightful inheritance, so long withheld him by his minister the cardinal, marked the decisive return of princes everywhere to their due authority and power after an unsettled and often turbulent period of some twenty years; so, too, did Charles II's restoration to the throne so nearly usurped by the aspiring commoner Cromwell, the 'Lord Protector'.

> Oh Happy Age! Oh times like those alone
> By Fate reserv'd for Great *Augustus* Throne!
> When the joint growth of Armes and Arts foreshew
> The World a Monarch, and that Monarch *You*

wrote Dryden as the final flourish of his *Astraea Redux*, a poem to celebrate the 'Happy Restoration and return of His Sacred Majesty Charles the Second'. In Britain, as in France, the crises of authority and the civil commotions of the Frondes and the Civil War or Great Rebellion were over: the rival claims and privileges of nobility and gentry, the Parlement and Parliament, the clergy, bar and solid bourgeoisie, were settled or subdued by the royal determination to circumvent such crises in the future through a deliberate reversion to more traditional conceptions of authority and power. 'L'état c'est moi,' Louis is reputed to have said in answer to a civil servant's question and, apocryphal or not, the famous phrase makes the new position very clear.

The doctrine that kings are the living image of God on earth and that they are his viceroys and lieutenants was widely current in seventeenth-century Europe. So obsessive and controversial became the abstract definition of sovereignty and the problems inherent in its practical application, that they gradually brought about a shift of interest away from the religious concerns of preceding generations to issues of a more secular and overtly political nature. From the moment that Protestant consolidation and Counter-Reformation expansion achieved a state of precarious balance at the end of the Thirty Years War in 1648, the time was ripe for a return to those royal preoccupations which had already begun to loom large in the Renaissance days of Henry VIII, Francis I and Charles V, that fortunate prince who had inherited the dual empire of Germany and Spain only to lay the enormous burden down, disillusioned, in 1555. In France a theoretical definition of royal authority was worked out at the height of the Wars of Religion by an eminent legal thinker, Jean Bodin, whose *Six Livres de la République* appeared in 1576, and reached an even wider audience through a Latin version in 1591. His emphasis on the ruler's role as the Lord's Anointed was an Old Testament notion which even Protestants could share, and soon Bodin and his supporters had laid the basis of the official ideology which prevailed during the reign of Henry IV, that murdered grandfather to whom Louis XIV felt he owed so much, and who was posthumously depicted magnificently enjoying his own apotheosis in one of the twenty-one canvases painted by Rubens to adorn the palace of his royal widow, Marie de' Medici.

'Non est enim potestas nisi a Deo,' St Paul had ruled in Romans 13, that classic text. 'Let every soul be subject unto the higher powers. For there is no power but of God: the powers that be are ordained of God,' translated the Anglican scholars commissioned to produce the Authorized Version of the Bible for the Most High and Mighty Prince James the First, in 1611. The passage was to become a major religious prop to uphold the new-found delight of princes in their royal role: 'le métier de Roi est grand, noble, délicieux,' the French king observed, and who had better cause to know? But, before such a majestic statement could be made, rigorous moral training had to be undergone, as Louis XIV certainly knew from personal experience. For he who is born or sets himself up to govern others must first of all learn how to govern himself. And that is a harder task; for, while the former is mainly a simple matter of victory over external forces, a question of diplomacy and military strength, the latter is the infinitely more glorious triumph of reason over the passions, and of duty over inclination. The baroque conception of the absolute ruler wielding his authority and prerogative by divine right was one which carried glorious perquisites, but it was not a passport to unbridled tyranny and corrupt despotism, as is made clear by the major literary works devoted at the time to the splendours and tribulations of kingship. It is not surprising, given the historical background, that these all date back to the problematic mid-century years which marked such a significant watershed in the evolution of baroque thought and culture.

In 1647, the year of his martyr play *Saint-Genest*, Rotrou also produced his most deeply considered masterpiece, a royal tragedy entitled *Venceslas*. With his mock-Bohemian counterpart of Christmas carol fame Rotrou's Polish king has little more than rank and age in common, and his tragedy really turns on the taming of the mettlesome personality of his son. Licentious, self-assertive and spoilt, young Ladislas is a prince who resents his royal father's longevity and well-meant good advice. Love, ambition and self-indulgence lead him to flout the rules and conventions that control the behaviour of lesser mortals, and he allows himself to pursue a career of unbridled selfishness at the expense of his father's wise and trusted favourite, Duke Fédéric, and of his own upright and honourable younger brother, Prince Alexandre. In the good tradition of Spanish cloak-and-dagger drama of which Rotrou was so fond, both princes are in love with the same woman. Jealousy and mistaken identity at night lead to an irreparable misdeed: Ladislas kills his brother in Cassandre's apartment under the false impression that he is Fédéric, whom he has assumed to be his enemy and rival. Venceslas, aged and sensing the imminent approach of his own death, is left with only one son and heir — and he a criminal. Paternal affection urges punishment yet also mercy, impartial justice demands impartial rigour, reason of state counsels a less harsh verdict. Unable to pass any just sentence on his son, Venceslas listens to the voices of his daughter and his minister, and to the voices of nature and his people. All demand the preservation of the prince's life, and force on Venceslas the realization that in spirit he has already abdicated from his throne and its enormous responsibilities. The crown is ultimately of more importance than the head which wears it, as he tells his son:

> Your head must either fall or bear the crown,
> Your crime be punished, or receive a prize.
> The state wants you as king; the nation teaches me
> By wanting you to live, that it has tired of me.
> Since Justice is, for kings, the queen of virtues,
> To wish me unjust is to wish me gone.

So Venceslas's will to reign (and for kings that means the will to live) is eroded from the moment that a disparity appears between the state and his own royal ego. The abstract issue concerning absolute justice is identical, in this tragedy of kings, with the human dilemma. From the moment that, in the gripping last few minutes of the play, the royal hero steps down from his throne to hand his son the diadem and sceptre, the past is obliterated, and he can display human emotions once more:

> Sans peine je descends de ce degré suprême:
> J'aime mieux conserver un fils qu'un diadême
> Dessous un nouveau règne oublions le passé...

Venceslas, a king no longer, can become a father again, and, with the symbolically effective gesture which these words both evoke and accompany, he can discard his kingly role and leave the stage of pomp and politics to spend his final days lamenting Alexandre's death and preparing for his own in privacy and the solitude not of greatness but of obscurity.

The final scenes of this great play, in so many ways the ordered and controlled French counterpart of Shakespeare's disjointed masterpiece *King Lear*, are deeply moving on an intimate personal level comparatively rare in baroque literature. Yet on analysis it soon becomes evident that the anguish of the old king and the poignancy of his son's gradual awakening to the claims and duties of his royal calling and his better self are in fact direct consequences of Rotrou's singleminded and eloquent concentration on one central theme, the abstract theme of kingship. We are moved because Venceslas, when he attains his finest and most venerable moments, is already fast ceasing to be a king. At first he seemed to be an opinionated and domineering old man, but just as we are beginning to realize how wrong our first impressions may have been, we sense that for him, tragically, it is too late. And so, with consummate dramatic and psychological artistry, Rotrou achieves what no doubt was his aim: he makes his spectators share the role and undergo the experience of Prince Ladislas, late, he too, to appreciate his father's virtues; thus we are enabled to experience in the vicarious form of drama the harrowing ordeals of qualifying for a crown. It was experiences in many ways akin to those of Ladislas that all the great monarchs of the baroque age had to undergo: Louis during the Frondes and under the guidance of Mazarin (as his mother, Anne of Austria, put it, kings do not need to *study* history since they *live* it); Charles II in the vicissitudes of the Civil War and the long exile which followed his father's trial and execution; and Leopold I in the traumatic experience of being torn from his personal vocation for the church owing to the death of an elder brother, and of being compelled to assume an office which his shyness and ungainly features rendered doubly fearsome. Like Ladislas in Rotrou's play, all three were young men of student age when they had to undergo their royal crises; and it is to readers of their age that a play such as *Venceslas* has the most immediate emotional appeal and perhaps also the greatest intellectual relevance.

Kingship and the limits of authority have been called the major intellectual issue of the baroque age. What subject, then, was better suited to the requirements of serious drama than the tragic conflicts associated with abdication and accession, especially when the theorists of literature were unanimous in their view that the characters in tragedy should be kings, queens and persons of high estate. Aristotle in his *Poetics* had merely suggested that tragedy was a representation of people who are better than the average; this new insistence on equating innate nobility and dignity with social station is therefore culturally significant as an indication of the growing importance which was being attached to rank and office. Understandably enough it followed that if a tragic hero was to be truly admired, he ought to be of more than noble birth or station; it was not until the advent of neoclassicism in the mid-eighteenth century that Aristotle's original definition was once again inter-preted without the social implications which had gathered around it after the publication of such seminal books as Julius Caesar Scaliger's *Seven Books on Poetics* (1561), a Latin survey of the art and craft of writing which rapidly acquired authoritative inter-national status. The transformation of what had been a helpful recommendation suggested by the practice of the ancient Grek tragic poets Sophocles and Euripides into a fully fledged and seldom questioned literary dogma with far-reaching social implic-ations is an excellent illustration of the convergence of political trends and poetic theory in the mid-seventeenth century. Tragedy, described by Martin Opitz, most influential theorist and poet in baroque Germany, as the most majestic branch of literature alongside epic poetry, was bound to be concerned increasingly with kings since it was an entertainment intended for the pleasure and improvement of a public which much enjoyed watching the splendours and vicissitudes of those whom it most admired and revered. The so-called *Haupt- und Staatsaktionen* of seventeenth-century Germany, blood and thunder melodramas about the fates of states and crowned heads which strolling players originally of English origin performed to gaping crowds in the market-places of provincial towns, provide a crudely vivid example of a taste which was shared by all levels of baroque society in Europe. They are in fact a popular, down-to-earth counterpart of the majestic dramatic debates on precisely the same topics — the destinies of sovereigns and empires — to which Corneille, the most brilliant dramatist in France, began to turn in 1640 with *Cinna*, a political drama which was to remain a great favourite with king, court and public until the imperial vision it evoked turned into a living reality around 1660.

Cinna is comparable to *Venceslas*, but it approaches the problem of kingship from a different angle. Unlike Rotrou's 'modern' play, which captured a dim reflection of contemporary dynastic conflicts in distant Poland, Corneille's drama works within a framework of references which link it more closely to the Italianate baroque tradition of Roman grandeur restored and also, paradoxically, to the anti-Italian and anti-baroque trends which were later to culminate in the rejection of Bernini and Cavalli by the French court and its artistic advisers, in favour of a consciously French brand of noble and sophisticated Augustan classicism. For Corneille's play, soon to become one of the epitomes of French classical culture, turns on the Roman emperor Augustus and the moral and political crisis which for two hours or so — the time the play takes to perform — he is obliged to undergo before he can, in the final scene, utter those proud and resonant words:

> Je suis maître de moi comme de l'univers;
> Je le suis, je veux l'être,

and hold out his hand in an equally memorable gesture to Cinna, the aspiring young favourite who has unsuccessfully plotted against him, saying 'Soyons amis, Cinna. . .' The confident tone, the serene poise, the almost colloquial simplicity of such words and actions are of course what has given the play its reputation as a masterpiece of classicism rather than a great classic. Yet it is said that Napoleon, no mean exponent of the imperial role, was always unhappy about the idealized, too-good-to-be-true dénouement of a drama which he otherwise greatly admired, until one day a professional actor brought home to him the fact that, when Augustus proffers his disarming invitation to his erstwhile enemy, he is actually dissembling his political intentions with all the astuteness of an experienced ruler — playing his part, in fact, upon the stage of Roman history. Perhaps Napoleon and the actor had a better understanding of the play than did professional critics: it is certainly very much in line with the general trends and thinking of the 1640s, that age of masks and dissimulation, civil unrest and political ambition, when France was governed by Corneille's patron Cardinal Richelieu. The cardinal had himself declared 'Savoir dissimuler est le savoir des rois'. Can the true motivations of Corneille's fictitious Augustus ever be known any better than the motives underlying the words and gestures of any prominent figure in a position of responsibility and in the public eye?

An age prone to disenchantment, uncertain of its values, and ready to question the credibility of its leading public figures, is likely to respond more readily to a baroque *Cinna* than to the classical reading of the play. In both cases the text remains exactly the same, and the emperor loses nothing of his majesty whether his words to Cinna are sincere or not. His appalling visions of the

untold bloodshed that led to his assumption of absolute power ring
true enough; significantly they are expressed in the intimate and
confidential form of monologue, about which Corneille usually had
reservations because it seemed to him to be such an unrealistic
device. But not so in *Cinna*, where public and private motivations
are inextricably mixed and where the problems inherent in its
conciliatory classical ending should not obscure the rich baroque
allusiveness with which Augustus opens Act III. For here Corneille's
Roman emperor actually gives voice to a conception of royal
disenchantment which is in every detail compatible with the
characteristic themes and outlook of contemporary baroque writers
in other parts of Europe. Grandiose and majestic in style and
delivery, yet deeply imbued with a sense of the dangers of fawning
flattery and hollow praise, their dark stoical resignation interrupted
by flashes of ephemeral brightness, these are the words of a true
baroque sovereign about to undergo the testing ordeal of discovering that his most trusted friend has turned against him. They are a
confirmation that this world is indeed an unstable, miserable place;
yet this insight acts as a spur to greater nobility of action and to an
almost superhuman display of heroic self-assertion:

> Cet empire absolu sur la terre et sur l'onde,
> Ce pouvoir souverain que j'ai sur tout le monde,
> Cette grandeur sans bornes et cet illustre rang,
> Qui m'a jadis coûté tant de peine et de sang,
> Enfin tout ce qu'adore en ma haute fortune
> D'un courtisan flatteur la présence importune,
> N'est que de ces beautés dont l'éclat éblouit,
> Et qu'on cesse d'aimer sitôt qu'on en jouit.

Recognition of the vanity of earthly pomp and rejection of
worldly power and splendour in an eloquent gesture of profound
disdain, yet at the same time a proud reassertion of absolute
authority in a grand display of the royal prerogative of clemency:
these may at first seem to be mutually incompatible. But they
certainly were not incompatible in an age which could equate kings
with God and delight in conferring the title of 'King of Kings' upon
the Almighty, while at the same time also glorying in depictions of
His degradation in the Crucifixion and death of Christ. Nor was
there a king in Europe whose way to the throne had not led him
through the sombre pomps of his predecessor's obsequies and who

had not witnessed the ceremonial associated with royal funerals. 'Let us to death in solemn triumph go': the towering catafalques draped in sable cloth blazed with countless candles, and slow processions wound to solemn music like that composed by Purcell for the funeral of Queen Mary in 1694. Perhaps, too, there would ring out a funeral oration such as the one delivered by Bossuet for Charles I's daughter Henrietta Stuart in 1670, which culminated in the awesome advice:

> Commencez aujourd'hui à mépriser les faveurs du monde; et, toutes les fois que vous serez dans des lieux augustes, dans ces superbes palais à qui Madame donnait un éclat que vos yeux recherchent encore. . . songez que cette gloire que vous admiriez faisait son péril en cette vie.

Never was bleak advice more resplendently put; but it was advice that was generally accepted in those days. The deaths of princes and princesses did indeed present a living lesson to humanity to despise the favours of this world and to realize that its august halls and superb palaces were no more than settings for those whose power and radiant personality had brought them to life. Sometimes these settings could even represent a serious moral danger by making this world appear to be a finer and more permanent place than it really is. However glorious the terrestrial lives of kings, they are in no way comparable to the glories of celestial life — that enormous bliss which so many of the painters, poets and musicians of the period attempted and sometimes almost succeeded in conveying. No wonder that characteristic gesture mingling heroic triumph and profound disdain!

'La grandeur et la gloire! Pouvons-nous encore entendre ces noms dans ce triomphe de la mort?' Bossuet asked the courtly congregation attending the obsequies of Louis XIV's sister-in-law Henrietta, that gifted princess who had done so much to cement the political alliance between France and Restoration England and to reconcile their divergent cultural traditions. No, continues Bossuet, grandeur and glory are high-sounding, bombastic words invented by arrogant men to dazzle themselves and deafen themselves to their own nothingness. For the body in the tomb will turn to dust and ashes, and finally become, in Bossuet's immortal phrase, 'un je ne sais quoi, qui n'a plus de nom dans aucune langue'. 'Peut-on bâtir sur ces ruines?' asks the preacher faced by the scenes of desolation he has evoked. 'Peut-on appuyer quelque grand dessin sur ce débris inévitable des choses humaines?' The rhetorical questions that well up in Bossuet's majestic funeral oration for the daughter of Charles I are ones which rise from the very heart of the European baroque. Self-esteem demolished, and grandeur obliterated by the triumph of death; glory, a concept reduced to an empty word; social distinctions nullified by the omnipotence of the divine; the tomb, an imposing reminder that man is nothing; and lastly, in the seeming despair of these insights, the telling architectural allusions to building upon ruins and basing grand designs upon a heap of rubble. The sequence of the argument reminds us that the period which produced some of the most ambitious and imposing building-projects ever undertaken was also deeply marked by an acute awareness of the instability and impermanence of all human endeavour.

It has sometimes been claimed, and with good reason, that Spain was the true home of the baroque. By the end of the sixteenth century its austere sense of religious purpose and its centralized autocratic government had been given solid symbolic substance in the palace-monastery of the Escorial (completed in 1584), from which the solitary Philip II ruled the immense and far-flung empire bequeathed him by Charles V. Spain's military might and wealth, its impassioned championship of Counter-Reformation values and its popular delight in stage and entertainment were some of the chief facets of a national culture which managed to hold in balance many of the spiritual and worldly contrasts associated with the baroque. But by the reign of Philip IV (1621-65) and the heyday of his favourite, Olivarez, whose appearances Velázquez captured in his famous portraits, Spain's power and influence were beginning to decline. Its cultural influence had been stimulating and colourful during the earlier phase of the baroque, but it never managed to recapture its appeal after the unsettled period in mid-century. By 1640 even Portugal and Catalonia had succeeded in shaking off Spanish rule. How low Spanish fortunes had sunk; how threadbare now was the glamour of Spanish cloak-and-dagger romance. In 1659 the decline of Spanish influence in Europe was marked by the marriage of Louis XIV to Philip's daughter; this was also the Italian Cardinal Mazarin's last and greatest contribution to the stability which Europe's central monarchies regained around 1600, and was in many ways to prove the prelude to the most opulent phase of the baroque. It was a phase to which Spain no longer had any significant contribution to make. In 1665 Philip IV died and was succeeded by the most impotent prince ever to rule a seventeenth-century kingdom: Spain's Charles II, whose imminent death was to keep Europe waiting until 1700, was a vivid embodiment of its decline, and quite incapable of projecting that heroic image which was now expected of a ruling prince.

Fortunate was the country in Europe after 1660 which found itself ruled by someone who could cut a glorious figure in the world. Indeed there are times when the success or failure of a nation to achieve a genuine high-baroque culture seems almost to have depended on its ruler's ability to project an appropriate image. To do this meant commissioning the right artists to radiate and perpetuate it and to create the setting for it. Versailles was gradually transformed from a modest hunting lodge, and magnified into the vast edifice which has ever since been regarded as the epitome of regal splendour. And all over Europe the same desire was at work to create settings commensurate with the now fashionable conception of kingship. So compelling was this urge, and so pre-eminently worthwhile did it seem, that any expense appeared justified and material obstacles could not be allowed to stand in its way — like the swamp and disease which threatened to hold up construction of Peter the Great's new residence and administrative centre of St Petersburg (founded in 1703). Enormous sums were spent, and the result was the 'royal palace' as generally understood, often with a whole town in attendance on it. No doubt its origins went back to the Italian Renaissance, to the French châteaux, and to descriptions of the vanished palaces of Roman antiquity such as Nero's Golden House and Hadrian's Tivoli. But one of the first clear tokens of what was to come was the Palace of the Luxembourg in Paris, built to suit the Franco-Italian taste of Marie de' Medici, and embellished with Rubens's twenty-one canvases extolling her career and virtues with supreme panache and visual flattery (1622-5). Such an achievement, ultra-modern when it was first seen, was to set the pattern for the period of regal and cultural centralization which came into force later in the century.

One of the most obvious characteristics of the baroque palace is that it is a building designed for peacetime. Gone is all trace of military fortification; there is scarcely even a sentry box or guardhouse, until you look more closely. The battlements and turrets of the late Middle Ages have almost disappeared; the moats are stylized into ornamental waters which, like the formal gardens, reflect the rituals that surround a sovereign's person. All over Europe palaces of this new kind arose, and none more elegant than those built for Christian IV in Denmark. But nowhere were they more numerous and nowhere did they flout economic laws and limitations more blatantly than in the innumerable states which together constituted the Holy Roman Empire. Every German prince required a palace, for each, though tributary, ruled in his own right. And those who considered themselves superior to the rest required palaces magnificent enough to justify their claims and satisfy their self-esteem. Thus the Electors, whose function it was to elect the Emperor (in fact they never exercised it throughout the high-baroque era, since Leopold reigned from 1658 to 1705), started building themselves town and country residences commensurate with their dignity and status, the Margrave of Brandenburg at Berlin, the Prince-Archbishop of Cologne at Brühl, and so on: Schloss Nymphenburg on the outskirts of Munich, begun in 1664 for the Elector of Bavaria, is a particularly impressive example. By 1697 the Emperor himself decided to commission his court architect Fischer von Erlach to construct that vast new palace which, after Versailles, is probably the best known of Europe's baroque palaces: Schönbrunn.

The craze reached England too. Charles II had visions of an equally splendid residence near Winchester; designed by Sir Christopher Wren, its windows would have looked out towards Spithead, symbol of England's naval power, and out across the Channel to those distant shores whose cultural and religious radiations the king could never bring himself to disregard. But this palatial dream never got much further than the drawing-board, and what little materialized of Britain's royal counterpart to Schönbrunn and Versailles was later on demolished. The Palace of Whitehall did not fare much better. At the request of Charles I Inigo Jones drew plans for the complete reconstruction of what was a medieval and Tudor hotchpotch, and at the Restoration his son revived the idea. But only one component of these large-scale Whitehall schemes got off the ground: the Banqueting House.

Its architectural style was already old-fashioned by European standards, for Inigo Jones designed it in the calm and static manner made famous by the Italian architect Palladio in the 1550s, but on its ceiling allegorical and mythological figures painted by Rubens in the early 1630s float with a baroque abandon unparalleled in England, though less flamboyant and less panegyrical than those in his canvases for the Dowager Queen of France. Design and decoration were to make this fine building a fitting backdrop for the greatest tragic royal act in seventeenth-century history, the execution of King Charles I.

The edifice which comes closest to the unfulfilled visions of Winchester and Whitehall and which in spirit and appearance most closely parallels the palaces of Europe is Blenheim, designed by Vanbrugh and begun in 1704, and offered by a grateful nation to its great military commander, the Duke of Marlborough, who with the Franco-Austrian Prince Eugene had won the War of the Spanish Succession after the death of Spain's miserable Charles II. Fought mainly on Belgian, German and Italian soil, it put an end at last to France's mounting predominance in Europe, so that the new century opened under the joint influence of Austria and Britain. And in many ways Blenheim Palace is a significant counterpart to the Belvedere Palace in Vienna, designed at the same time for Marlborough's military colleague Prince Eugene by Lucas von Hildebrandt. To compare the two is interesting. The Prince built his great house from his own funds and for his delectation, and achieved an effect of effervescent grandeur. The motive underlying the construction of Blenheim actually came closer to that which inspired the palaces of baroque kings, and makes it unique in England; it is a panegyric in stone, caught midway between static weightiness and dynamic movement, classical proportions and monumental exuberance. The purpose behind the erection of vast edifices like Blenheim was to extol the virtues and achievements of their owner. Panoplies and trophies in stone and plaster negligently thrown together to form eye-catching embellishments of aptly martial kind are thus a feature of this particular building, just as the symbols of the Sun-King and his solar cult have their intrinsic decorative part to play in the total design of Versailles, and the emblems of high ecclesiastical and political office adorn the imposing German palace built in 1711-21 at Pommersfelden to express the self-satisfaction felt by Lothar Franz von Schönborn, Archbishop and Elector of Mainz, Primate of Germany, Bishop of Bamberg and Lord High Chancellor of the Holy Roman Empire. Such inordinate rank and dignity required no less a show in the late baroque age.

The self-conceit evident in baroque palaces reflects their builders' view of themselves and the image they intended to project. But in order to laud and honour their names and magnify their deeds before all men, they also required the services of writers and artists who, throughout the period, were almost always ready to place their talents at the disposal not only of their sovereigns, but of rulers and princes, whoever they might be. Financial reasons naturally had a part to play in this readiness to sing the praises of kings and patrons: he who pays the piper calls the tune was a commonplace more relevant than ever in the period when Louis XIV's favourite musician, the Italian Lully, made the French court's musical establishment the envy of Europe and a model for the innumerable court orchestras which were in turn to affect the whole development of symphonic music in the eighteenth century. But so ubiquitous and long-lasting was the fashion for eulogy and pan-egyric, and so convincingly effective were some of its products, that one senses the presence of more profound and compelling cultural motives. It manifested itself in a flood of odes, cantatas, epitaphs and inscriptions in both Latin and the newer national tongues, addressed to potentates and princes, prelates and patrons, and praising their bounty, justice and martial valour, their piety or their munificence, as occasion demanded. Though designed and com-posed with half an eye on posterity, such works were essentially of and for the moment, and their sheer volume and prolixity enhances the impression that they were the period's favourite way of sustaining its mania for self-congratulation. Poetry and music of this kind, like the inscriptions on monuments and the epitaphs on tombs, have an inflated and hollow ring to the modern ear, and visually, too, the gestures and attendant paraphernalia seem overblown:

> Wrapt soft and warm your Name is sent on high,
> As flames do on the wings of Incense fly:
> Musique her self is lost, in vain she brings
> Her choisest notes to praise the best of Kings:
> Her melting strains in you a tombe have found,
> And lye like Bees in their own sweetnesse drown'd.
> He that brought peace and discord could attone,
> His Name is Musick of it self alone.

Thus wrote Dryden with almost preposterous high-baroque

fulsomeness in his *Panegyrick* on Charles II's coronation in 1661, yet almost meaning every honeyed word he said. Often the high-sounding words are both hackneyed and farfetched in an effort to avoid the risk of banal commonplace which by the late baroque period was threatening to dull what little meaning several decades of intensive use had left. As Bossuet warned, words such as grandeur and glory can sound like bombastic nonsense invented to dazzle us and blind us to the truth of our nothingness. By the early eighteenth century such words were understandably much devalued. Yet paradoxically there are times, as in Bossuet's own funeral orations, when the balance between meaning and hollowness, triumph and despair, is so finely caught that the age's characteristic desire to exalt its great men and their achievements can actually strike us as a heroic defiance of its sense of abject insecurity.

In the German-speaking world one of the most admired composers of epitaphs and eulogies in music was Johann Froberger, court organist to the Emperor Ferdinand III whose death in 1657 he deplored in a tensely melancholy keyboard lamentation. Another, famous for his prose funeral orations, was the dramatist and poet Gryphius. Both travelled widely, Froberger reaching London and Gryphius acquiring some distinction as a scholar and teacher at the Dutch University of Leyden, one of the principal centres of seventeenth-century learning. He was by no means ignorant of the achievements of contemporaries such as Vondel and Rembrandt, Corneille and Descartes. But it is characteristic of the cultural situation in Germany that he never became more than a figure respected by his immediate Silesian contemporaries and by his fellow German writers and poets. In vain he waited for a summons to the imperial court at Vienna, where the musician Froberger worked; he knew better than we do now that such a call was most unlikely. For it was a corollary of the Empire's complicated make-up that no decisive centralization of cultural forces could ever take place. Instead of being concentrated in a centre of taste and fashion, a meeting-place for everyone that mattered, like London, Paris or Madrid, the high society of seventeenth-century Germany, its nobility and clergy, its vast array of functionaries and officials, and all their wives and daughters, were shared out between the courts and capitals (the *Residenzen*) of its many semi-independent rulers; and with them went the artists, poets and composers too. Most of these rulers were intent on fostering their own interests rather than those of the Empire, and spent enormous sums of money to that end; and the resultant social and cultural pattern was made doubly intricate because the sixteenth-century axiom 'Cujus regio eius religio' still by and large held true. The German states were Lutheran, Calvinist or Roman Catholic according to the religion of their rulers. The Habsburgs being by tradition Catholic, great sums were lavished on Vienna where as emperors they resided, so as to make it at least a centre of Catholic activity and culture, and thus a model for lesser places sharing the same religious faith. Despite his imperial loyalties, Gryphius belonged to the other camp, and the Thirty Years War had exacerbated such distinctions.

The particularization and virtual disintegration of the state which in France Henry IV, Richelieu and Louis XIV actually succeeded in averting, and which in the 1640s even threatened to undermine the monolithic unity of Spain and disrupt Britain, were thus an integral feature of baroque Germany. And it may not have been so detrimental as later historians have liked to think. The extraordinary thing is that, despite the devastation of the Thirty Years War, in its later stages fought mainly to further the interests of foreign states, Germany was able to generate enough cultural energy to keep artistic and musical activity alive in so many widely separated centres, from city-states like Breslau, a proud burgher republic in the eastern province of Silesia, to Salzburg in Austria, administered and embellished by its proudly munificent prince-bishops. Or Würzburg and Bamberg, both containing palaces and churches worthy of the wealthiest and most cultivated kingdoms, and designed and decorated by the leading artists of the day. Such undertakings had to be paid for, as had the services of the musicians and painters: J. S. Bach, for instance, composing his celebrated 'Sheep may safely graze' as part of a secular 'Hunting Cantata' to celebrate the birthday of Duke Christian of Saxe-Weissenfels in 1716, or the Venetian Tiepolo, summoned to Catholic Würzburg in 1750 to paint the supreme example of visual self-glorification on the ceilings of the prince-bishop's palace at a time when most of Western Europe had moved on from the baroque to the totally alien climate of the Enlightenment and the Age of Reason.

Baroque Vienna was unable to command the cultural and financial resources of an entire realm in the way that Paris or even London could. In this respect, too, the imperial role was that of *primus inter pares*, a relative superiority among equals which could only be kept up by lavish expenditure, the funds often being provided in good

Habsburg tradition by a network of matrimonial alliances, dowries and legacies. One of these enabled Leopold I to stage the many months of almost non-stop celebration which marked his marriage to his niece, the Infanta Margarita Teresa in 1666, the dynastic marriage which prompted Lohenstein's *Sophonisbe*, a tragedy of imperial conflicts and ambitions, and the construction of the gigantic opera house Auf der Cortina. For many contemporaries, however, the climax of the celebrations was the firework display, when some 22,000 rockets, firecrackers and squibs exploded to proclaim that the hearts of Jupiter, the demigod Hercules and all loyal subjects were aflame with affection for the imperial couple. Public entertainment and state occasion fused in evanescent brilliance to highlight the imperial ideal; the organizers must have thought their funds well spent.

In England royal expenditure on the baroque priorities of self-glorification and self-indulgence were limited in much the same way as were the powers and prerogatives of the crown. A parliamentary system is by nature incompatible with the baroque, and doubly so in an increasingly middle-class and anti-Catholic country like England. Indeed, is baroque culture truly possible in a non-Catholic environment? The answer is, only to a limited extent. Without the presence of the Catholic faith or the proximity and example of its adherents, it is an artistic and literary ideal both elusive and in the end, perhaps, unworkable. This is why the 'baroque' art and literature of England bear a similar relationship to their Continental counterparts as the Anglican church did to the church of Rome. The Act of Uniformity which came into force in 1662 succeeded in establishing the system of one church throughout the realm in place of the multiplicity of sects and forms of worship in the Commonwealth period. To this extent it represented an attitude comparable to Louis XIV's distaste for all religious views which smacked of anarchy and threatened the central authority of himself, the state. The difference was, of course, the fact that the Act of Uniformity was designed to enforce the supremacy of a Protestant church and not that of Roman Catholicism, which was so dominant a factor in the evolution of the baroque, and which the English king is said to have cherished in his secret heart. Attempts to bridge this gap had unfortunate results, as James II discovered when British reactions to his fervent Roman Catholic inclinations forced him to realize that, unlike Louis XIV, he could not claim that sovereign and state were one and indivisible.

In England a revolution was considered preferable to an authoritarian and pro-Catholic king. The events of 1688, when taken in conjunction with those of 1649 and 1660, demonstrate that shared values in the domains of taste, art, politics and even religion were not quite strong enough to bring about a fully convincing flowering of high-baroque culture in England comparable with what was taking place on the continent of Europe. Political developments and a centralized government curtailed the freedom of the British high nobility to glory in its provincial independence, while the temper and function of the Anglican church made an English Würzburg quite unthinkable. This is what makes Blenheim Palace, erected to honour one man with monies voted by parliament, into such a significant exception. No wonder Britain's cultural relationship with baroque Europe is such a vexed and complicated one. When Charles I commissioned Rubens to paint the apotheosis of his father, James I, on the ceiling of Inigo Jones's Banqueting House and knighted him in recognition of his services, it was quite clear that England was being drawn into the mainstream of European culture; and many other trends in church and state — like the love of lavish masques and high church ritual, the reliance on royal favourites, and the neglect of parliamentary government — pointed in the same direction. The Civil War that resulted can thus also be seen in broader terms as the manifestation of a cultural crisis which turned, with apt significance, on the problem of the king, his role and function. No wonder, too, that these events were watched by Europe with the spellbound gaze of an audience in a theatre. They were a tragedy of state in true baroque manner, a *Haupt- und Staatsaktion* in which the characters were real and important figures, not strolling English players.

In August 1644 Andreas Gryphius, on his way from Holland to Rome, witnessed the arrival of Queen Henrietta Maria of England in the French town of Angers, where she had fled on a Dutch boat after the royalist defeat on Marston Moor. The sight of this proud child of Henry IV and Marie de' Medici, a fugitive from her own realm and subjects, aroused feelings in the German poet which reveal the supranational qualities of baroque thinking when sovereigns and kingship were concerned:

By kings begotten and of royal birth,
Whom kings adored, and who in tender years

Was wedded to a king, to kings gave birth
When kingdoms three had chosen to crown her Queen —
You now, glad Angers, see in deepest woe...

But then the emphatic formality of the panegyric gives way, in a
manner characteristic of this poet, to a closer scrutiny of his
subject's features in an attempt to read the moral lesson written by
events. The tone of voice alters, and so too does the style. The
formal portrait, the celebrated profile by Van Dyck, turns to look at
us with the grave poignancy of a Rembrandt:

Gaze on the majesty playing in her eyes,
The features which reveal the cares they feel,
And learn that what's high-born must suffer greater fears.

Few English speakers know that the tragic gaze of Charles's queen
fell on a great German poet who was ready to see in her, as so many
contemporaries did, the virtues of her courageous father, Henry IV
of France, who had been assassinated some months after her birth;
virtues recapitulated with all the fervour of formal grief by Bossuet
when he drew a 'picture, albeit imperfect' of her in the funeral
oration he delivered in 1669:

O mère! ô femme! ô reine admirable! et digne d'une meilleure
fortune, si les fortunes de la terre étaient quelque chose; enfin il
faut céder à votre sort...

for the fortunes of this world are as nothing: they are like a gilt
surface concealing the inexorable decrees of fate. Like a column
supporting the huge mass of a crumbling temple, the queen, says
Bossuet, had tried to uphold the state when it was at the mercy of
invincible forces. Now all that is left is to stand fast amid the ruins.
And, once again, the imagery of architecture, of Roman temple
and of crumbling glory, is used to convey the stark lessons of life
and death. It was imagery readily understandable to people who
were trying to re-create the splendours of imperial Rome, and who
used the broken pillar as a motif on their tombs.

Gryphius recorded his first response to what was taking place in
Britain in his sonnet to the queen. But when in February 1649 news
reached the Continent of the king's execution, his creative reaction
was immediate and intense. Soon the first draft of a sombre
political tragedy was ready. *Carolus Stuardus* is the seventeenth

century's most sustained dramatic study of the functions and meaning of kingship. It presents in stylized form the events of the last twelve hours before the execution, and with measured pace charts its royal hero's progress through this vale of tears to meet his Maker: his way, too, from the dignified resignation of his long monologues in captivity and his farewells to family and advisers, to his triumphant, almost operatic last appearance on the scaffold, there to act out his tragic royal part against the backdrop of the Banqueting House in Whitehall. While Gryphius in Breslau was writing this royalist play, Andrew Marvell composed his great political poem, the *Horatian Ode upon Cromwell's Return from Ireland* (1650), in which he too sets that 'memorable scene' and talks of the 'Royal Actor' adorning the 'tragic scaffold', all within the rich texture of apt allusions to both contemporary Britain and ancient Rome. It is this visual and essentially dramatic nucleus that Gryphius takes, expanding it to embrace the whole wide range of spiritual, political and legal issues which the execution of the king raised in his mind and in those of the small but widely dispersed number of cultivated Germans for whom he was writing. To them the 'Murder of the King's Majesty' (as the play is subtitled) was a ritual and judicial killing comparable to that of Christ, and carried out in defiance of the indisputable fact that a king is the earthly embodiment of divinely instituted order, the headspring of the laws to which his people are subject, and answerable to God alone, by whose grace he enjoys his royal authority. As the action of the tragedy moves relentlessly forward towards its foregone conclusion, Gryphius's concern moves from the specifically British issues — parliamentary prerogatives; forms of religious observance; Anglo-Scottish tensions, and so on — and shifts to its European repercussions. These are discussed in the play by the Dutch and German diplomatic representatives in London, who see them as a warning to the rulers of Europe, a prelude to another war, and a foretaste of social, moral and religious upheaval. 'Anarchy is nothing else but a broken monarchy, where every man is his own monarch,' wrote Sir Robert Filmer in 1652, and the symbolic act of 30 January 1649, in which the person of the king was physically broken, had a deeply disturbing message for the European nations which had just concluded the Peace of Westphalia (24 October 1648) and put an end to the fragmentation of the Thirty Years War. Were the ghosts of that war — the unhappy 'Winter King'

(Charles's brother-in-law), the ambitious, murdered Wallenstein —
really quite laid? The king's last word was 'Remember!' The royal
splendours of high-baroque Europe were to be haunted by the
spectre of the Stuart martyr-king who in death achieved the
apotheosis which, in life, Rubens had given his father.

The execution of Charles I made such a deep impression because it
was an event unique in seventeenth-century Europe. It says much for
the respect in which royalty was held that throughout the baroque
period no other prominent ruler met with a violent end. The
assassination in 1610 of Henry IV of France by a Roman Catholic
fanatic wa a last flicker of that late Renaissance (or Jacobean) violence
and passion which had provoked the murders of Henry III of France
(1589) and William the Silent of the Netherlands (1584), as well as
the captivity and execution of Mary Queen of Scots (1587) to whom
Vondel had just devoted a tragedy fittingly dedicated to the Winter
King's son (1645). Such outrages were entirely out of keeping with
the new era's conception of absolute monarchy. By the late 1650s it
had become both safe and usual for monarchs to dine in public, to
walk about among their subjects, and to admit all comers of quality
to their parks and palaces. Indeed Louis XIV, remembered as the
incarnation of haughty majesty, was in the habit of conversing
affably with everyone he met and of greeting all members of the
fairer sex with the courtesy characteristic of the 'First Gentleman of
France' — conduct which would be the despair of security officials in
more modern times. But, secure in the sense of royal dignity which
they shared with all their subjects, the high-baroque princes had
scant need for security: a ceremonial guard of honour was usually
enough.

The sacrosanct position of the European monarch in the later
seventeenth century was not achieved without effort, as Rotrou's
Venceslas had shown. Not only was it considered imperative to
educate princes in the art of ruling and for the tasks of government —
a tradition that went back to the Renaissance and far beyond; it was
also increasingly typical of the new ethos of absolutism for princes to
sever their connections with lesser mortals or at least to confine their
personal attentions to their mistresses, their regiments, their dogs
and horses. Queens, for example, ceased to play the dominant roles
to which they had been accustomed; Marie de' Medici and Henrietta
Maria had tried to play an active part in politics, to be queens in their
own right; but Marie-Thérèse and Catherine of Braganza were no

more than pallid figures overshadowed by their husbands and their husbands' mistresses, while the three wives of Leopold I made no mark at all on history and left no memories behind them. The monolithic nature of the baroque throne did not allow more than one person to sit upon it, and the baroque conception of service to the state presupposed that no man can obey two masters. This theme was powerfully treated by Gryphius in 1659 in his monumental tragedy *Papinianus*, which dramatizes the violent rivalry between Caracalla and Geta, brothers and heirs to the Roman emperor Severus, who cannot bear to share the glory of the imperial throne they have both inherited. The outcome — the triumph of the more determined of the two, despite the moral reservations of their tutor Papinianus — was a timely and rueful recognition of the moral losses entailed by absolutism, the period's dominant political trend. There was a further aspect of this new ethos which was perhaps even more important. Essential to the emergence of a new and idealized conception of absolute kingship was the rejection of that long-standing phenomenon, the royal favourite, which had become so influential in the culture of the sixteenth century. It was not surprising that this phenomenon had appealed to writers and audiences in the early baroque period, in which people had seen the gradual rise and sudden fall of favourites such as the Duke of Buckingham, assassinated in 1628, and the Count-Duke of Olivarez, who dominated Philip IV of Spain until 1643. The struggle between aspiring, self-conceited favourites and selfless, modest advisers for the hearts and consciences of princes was a theme which only started to lose its popularity when its topical relevance receded.

Emphasis on the divinity of princes was also bound to make the notion of rebellion take on deeper meaning:

> What King, what Crown from Treasons reach is free,
> If *Jove* and *Heaven* can violated be?

asks Dryden in his poem *Astraea Redux*, and indeed the notion of rebellion, a vexed issue for all, was anathema to many. From the extreme edges of the religious spectrum came views which provoked the outraged disagreement of the majority who held fast to the doctrine enshrined in the second verse of Romans 13, 'Whosoever therefore resisteth the power, resisteth the ordinance of God: and they that resist shall receive to themselves damnation.' But on the Calvinist flank the German jurist Johannes Althusius put forward a neostoic theory to the effect that the people have the right to rise up against a tyrannical ruler (*Politica methodice digesta*, 1603). On the Spanish Jesuit side Juan de Mariana went so far as to advance arguments which seemed to favour tyrannicide (*De rege et regis institutione*, 1604) and which were blamed for inspiring both the assassination of Henry IV and the Gunpowder Plot against James I. The repercussions of such views were naturally felt throughout the early part of the century and culminated in the spate of rebellions and disturbances which marked its central years. Not only in France and England; in Naples the anti-Spanish uprising associated with the fisherman Masaniello flared up in 1647, in the Ukraine a Cossack revolt shook the Polish state to its foundations, Portugal and Catalonia had their troubles, and even in far-off Istanbul a mutiny resulted in the murder of Sultan Ibrahim in 1648. Questions arose. What is rebellion? And what, if any, is its justification? These were the questions which thinking men were asking in mid-century, and which inspired the creation of the great imaginative depictions of rebellion which are the outstanding literary masterpieces of those torn and turbulent years, Vondel's *Lucifer* (1654) and Milton's *Paradise Lost* (1667).

Milton started to turn his earlier drafts for a drama on the Fall of Man into an epic poem in 1658. Some years before, Vondel had seen the usually tolerant Amsterdam authorities put a stop to the production of his drama *Lucifer*, despite its audience's applause, though not to the seven printings which this, the greatest work in Dutch, enjoyed in its first year. Vondel had been roused to indignation by events in England and, as was usual with him, emotion set alight that creative passion which then welled up and soared to extraordinary baroque heights in a solemn, formal drama on nothing less than the rebellion and subsequent fall of Satan and his angels. There is one thing Vondel's angel cannot bear, and that is to come second. He thirsts for pride of place and, hearing from one of his angelic henchmen an eye-witness account of newly created paradise and the enormous bliss of Adam and Eve, mere mortals, his envy knows no bounds. The news that God has decided to become incarnate in human form is the last straw:

> Mankind has won God's heart and is now Heaven's friend!
> For angels, night has fallen: our servitude begins.

So Lucifer, the morning star, decides to defy the divine decree:

> 'Tis just to win
> The highest place; to attempt, yet fail, is sin!

His deliberate insistence on the insignia of majesty at this point is unmistakable:

> And if I needs must fall, bereft of rank and honour,
> Then let me fall with, on my head, this crown,
> This sceptre in my fist, this trusty guard of honour...
> Far rather be the first in any lesser court'
> Than second here, or less.

Vast distances of cosmic action have to be crossed in this most spacious of baroque dramas before once-mighty Lucifer can at last give vent to his tragic anguish in the speech that expresses to perfection the experience of all who, in their pride, rebel only to realize that their action is futile:

> Was ever creature born more miserable than I?

he asks himself as the stark awareness dawns that

> There is no going back; no, we have climbed too high.
> What now? What's to be done in such extremity?
> Time suffers no delay — if time's the proper name
> For this brief space between salvation and damnation.

Caught thus in what Vondel calls the 'insufficiency' of time and totally unable to rethink his fatal step, he hears the trumpet sound: the final showdown is upon him. As the glorious triumph of the Almighty's army is acclaimed by all the hosts of heaven around the throne (fit subject for a painted baroque ceiling!), Lucifer takes on before our eyes the hideous form of a monstrous serpent, to be hurled down from the outermost verge of heaven in a last encounter with the archangel Michael — ironically to gain the satisfaction of revenge by sliding into Eden and seducing Eve and Adam in their innocent bliss. Milton apart, no other poet of the baroque period could achieve the audacious feat of paraphrasing the dynamic swirl of colour, light and movement with which Rubens had conveyed the cosmic battle of good and evil in his small and large *Last Judgments* and *Fall of the Damned*, painted between 1617 and 1620.

On the fringes of the Catholic baroque world of absolute kings and sacred monarchy, Vondel and Milton between them evoked a picture of the anarchy of thought and chaos of the mind which was so convincing that in this respect alone their poems bear striking witness to the general desire for order in all spheres of life. Formal in both their structure and their diction, controlled and measured despite the colour and violence of their action and the improbability of their matter in the everyday, down-to-earth sense, their enormous dramatic epics, like Rubens's paintings, convey a passionate desire to see infinity in relation to their own time. But if one turns, for instance, to the angelic choruses which end each act of *Lucifer* by solemnly singing the praises of Almighty God, it becomes clear that on this higher, more spiritual level too, the baroque conception of power, order and sovereignty was inseparable from the baroque taste for eulogy and panegyric, and from that atmosphere of ambivalently fulsome praise with which its monarchs liked to surround themselves. The courts of Satan and the Lord Almighty are baroque courts seen in the imagination; and this is why their splendours ring so true.

7

All for love

Diana and Venus, those tutelary deities of the baroque world, presided over the lavish entertainments which inaugurated the park and gardens of Versailles in the May of 1664. Their official purpose was to honour those Spanish Habsburg ladies, Anne of Austria, the young king's mother, and Marie-Thérèse, his wife. But there was another reason for the *Plaisirs de l'île enchantée*. It was common knowledge at court that Louis was as much addicted to the pleasures of love as he was to the chase; and it was known that the real beneficiary of so much gallant inventiveness was his coy mistress, Louise de la Vallière.

Aristocratic circles are often prone to blasé disenchantment. But on this occasion the court of France allowed itself to be swept away for seven days on a wave of open-air merrymaking: cavalcades, carousels, masques, ballets and collations. Appropriately the idea underlying the *Plaisirs de l'île enchantée* was taken by its designer, the expatriate Italian Carlo Vigarani, from an episode in *Orlando furioso*, the well-known Italian mock-heroic Renaissance epic. Its author, the courtier-poet Ariosto, had transformed the medieval world of courtly romance into a world of modern make-believe; a world just heroic and gallant enough to appeal to high-born ladies, yet with sufficient irony and wit to recommend it to gentlemen too. Though a long-established classic (it first appeared in 1516), Ariosto's dazzling poem continued to exert its magic. Now, once again, its popularity was demonstrated as the French court, increasingly the arbiter of European fashion, set out to re-create its mood in contemporary terms. Why were they all so eager to participate in the synthetic pleasures of an enchanted island? Escapism? Or was it because they welcomed it as an image of their own privileged reality? It is hard to say in the case of this almost legendary high-baroque attempt to fuse the present with mythology in order to celebrate a way of life which made a virtue of such ambivalence.

There had been royal mistresses before. Indeed the courts of Renaissance Europe had brought the phenomenon to high perfection and endowed it with an aura of propriety which became increasingly essential with the rise of the new conceptions of morality and social order associated with baroque monarchy. And from the remoter days of imperial Rome the figure of Nero's mistress Poppaea survived as a prototype to which the baroque age felt particularly drawn. Poppaea's triumphant rise to political influence through her erotic wiles and sexual charms had dominated Seneca's tragic play *Octavia*; complementing as it did the ambitions and lusts of her lover Nero, it made an ideal subject for Monteverdi's most impressive large-scale achievement in secular music, the opera *L'Incoronazione di Poppea*, written for Venice in 1642. And later, at the time of the grandiose diversions at Versailles, this same Roman object-lesson in the potency of erotic and political forces became the unifying theme of two close-linked German tragedies by Lohenstein. *Agrippina* and *Epicharis*, both published in 1665, share many of the preoccupations and qualities of Monteverdi's opera. Above and beyond the general affinity which baroque Europe felt for imperial Rome, they represent an increasingly compelling fascination for the close relationship between political and erotic passion, and demonstrate the effects of both on a ruler still inexperienced in the arts of statesmanship. When in 1669 Racine turned his rapidly maturing mastery of close tragic form to the sudden death of Nero's first important victim, his brother-in-law Britannicus, he too was therefore on characteristic baroque ground; the originality of *Britannicus* was, however, that it dramatized the birth of a monster with little or no recourse to the stylistic and figurative devices which are such a dominant feature of other seventeenth-century Nero dramas. For the actor-emperor Nero, that travesty of the ideal ruler, with his histrionic desire to play the leading part upon the stage of life, was a figure that called out for dramatic treatment in the baroque period.

Monteverdi, Lohenstein and Racine are alike in the emphasis they lay on Nero's moral tutor Seneca — none other than the Roman philosopher-dramatist whose own *Octavia* and other plays were the prototype for their conception of serious, tragic drama. Seneca's historically authenticated failure to deflate Nero's self-conceit and curb his lusts amounts, of course, to a questioning of the period's favourite philosophy, neostoicism, and its ability to subdue the dual forces of love and ambition. In isolation and apart, both love and ambition are governable passions and can be used to good advantage; each involves intrinsic and ultimately preponderant virtues. Justice, clemency and a highly developed sense of personal honour are the stock attributes both of heroic rulers and of heroic lovers. But when united and impelled by selfishness and lust or by the drift of historical events, love and ambition are uncompromising; Nero and Poppaea are absolutely ruthless in their pursuit of personal fulfilment. An alliance such as theirs can be an unholy one indeed, and may well refuse to respect the moral and social impediments represented by more hallowed and conventional ties. Thus Nero has to overcome the domineering influence of his mother, Agrippina, and is seen to do so in all these baroque versions. Maternal control removed, his legal consort, Octavia, has to be ousted in Poppaea's favour. In other words, mother and wife represent obstacles in themselves beyond the emotional claims they make as individual human beings. The ties of filial piety and matrimony are social conventions which Christian morality had rendered sacrosanct. To see them broken by an emergent tyrant as an initial demonstration of his lust for personal power as sexual fulfilment was a shock to civilized susceptibilities. Its impact was captured in the poignant lament which Monteverdi and his librettist Busenello gave to Nero's deserted wife Octavia in their Venetian opera, a lament which raises questions almost too terrible to be voiced:

> Jove, listen to me;
> If you have no thunderbolts to punish Nero,
> I accuse you of being impotent and unjust.
> But, alas, I go too far, and I repent my thought:
> I must suppress my torment and bury it
> In unspoken anguish.

Were thoughts like this being entertained by some of those

present in the gardens of Versailles in 1664? If so, they were silenced by the noble noise of Lully's band as it accompanied the masques and ballets for which the fashionable pastoral poet Benserade had written elegant lyrics in mythological and bucolic vein, or they were lost among the courtiers' acclamations as Louis won a tilting match or danced a royal measure. Yet there were parallels for all to see, not least of them being the presence of France's two queens and the timid Louise de la Vallière, still so unused to the new and ambiguous station from which she would in a few years herself be ousted by the more self-confident charms of Madame de Montespan, the most complete embodiment of the new age's ideal. It is said that Louis XIV gave up dancing on detecting the innuendo which Racine had slipped into some lines of his *Britannicus* of 1669, where Nero's glorious exploits are extolled, but in ironic terms:

> His one ambition and his only merit
> Is to excel at driving racing chariots;
> He aspires to prizes quite unworthy of him,
> Displays himself before the Roman public,
> And shows his voice off in the theatre, hoping
> The audience will idolize him. Meanwhile soldiers
> Are busy goading them to more applause.

The ruler as performing artist before a captive and obsequious audience, as a virtuoso in the sphere of social entertainment as well as in his true domain of kingship, was a prospect which exerted very strong temptation in a period that set such store by art and spectacle. The audacity displayed by Racine, a supremely gifted artist, when he dared to include this aspect of Nero's conduct in *Britannicus*, is astounding, especially as his drama shares with its baroque counterparts that obsessive concern with the interplay of erotic and political motives which had always been associated with the figure of the tyrant. But at least there is no Poppaea here; she has not yet stepped on to the tragic scene of history any more than had the incomparable Françoise-Athenais de Mortemart de Roche-chouart, Marquise de Montespan, whose intimate relationship with her sovereign had not yet attracted public attention.

Nevertheless Racine's tragedy pulsates with erotic excitement. From the start, its claustrophobic atmosphere exploits to spine-chilling effect the static, impersonal décor demanded of French

tragedy by rigid aesthetic conventions which were respected as
religiously as those governing social life at court. The action of the
play takes place in a room in Nero's palace, an antechamber leading
to the emperor's personal apartments where, as the curtain rises,
Agrippina, his mother, is waiting before dawn, impatient for her
son to provide an explanation for the outrage that has just occurred
at dead of night: Junie, the protégée she has planned to marry to
her promising stepson Britannicus, has been carried off by force.
But by whom? On whose orders? Why? In this nightmare world of
palace corridors and antechambers, motives are obscure and
ambiguous and the reasons prompting action are apt to assume less
rational explanations once action itself is under way. Nero confides
to his fawning adviser:

Néron	Narcisse, c'en est fait, Néron est amoureux.
Narcisse	Vous?
Néron	Depuis un moment, mais pour toute ma vie. J'aime, que dis-je aimer! j'idolâtre Junie.

The passionate wit of this amorous confession then gives way to a
narration unparalleled for its pictorial richness and psychological
complexity, as Nero describes the experience which is transforming
him from a promising young prince into a lustful and infamous
despot:

> Excited by a curious desire, I watched her as she arrived here
> tonight, sad, and raising to the sky above her, eyes brimming
> with tears which sparkled among the torches and the weapons;
> lovely, unadorned, in the simple apparel of a beautiful woman
> just roused from sleep. Can you blame me? Her disarray, the
> shadows, the torchlight, the shouting and the silence, and the
> fierce look of her proud ravishers, all enhanced the timid
> sweetness of her eyes....Ravished by the sight of her, I tried
> to speak, but my voice failed me. Motionless, seized by my
> astonishment, I let her pass...

And so the nocturnal vision vanishes, invisible to the spectator in
this play in accordance with the French theatrical convention that
action should not take place on the stage. Yet as a grandiose word-
painting worthy of the finest baroque painter, it is doubly effective,
and no defects of actor or producer can diminish it, provided Nero
can declaim it suitably. The action is evoked entirely by the words,

words which in their subtle relationships to each other describe not
just the event that has occurred, but also the psychological responses
of the watching Nero. The sight of the beautiful Junie's vulnerability
at the hands of his own soldiers kindles the erotic passion dormant in
him; yet paradoxically it is a vision of beauty mute and chaste in
essence, glimpsed amid the chiaroscuro of leaping flames and
shadow, its potent impact brought out in words that are at once a
spontaneous emotional response and a *tour de force* of embellished,
heightened language, clearly conscious of its visual and sensual
connotations. Never was Racine more richly baroque than here.

Nero, glimpsed in the first dawn of erotic passion by Racine, and
sipping the first drops of that despotic power which was soon to
intoxicate him, is the central and obsessionally commanding figure
in Lohenstein's two 'Roman' tragedies of 1665. Here, however, as
in Monteverdi's opera, the monster is full-grown and in command
of every aspect of the world around him. His opening words convey
his inordinate sense of his own greatness in hyperbolic images well
chosen for this egocentric purpose:

> The sun stands still before our radiance,
> Our power astounds the world, arrests its course!
> We have lost count of the triumphal arches
> Rome has erected for us. . . .

The first step, the murder of Britannicus, has already been taken,
and the darkness of Nero's horrid vices has already begun to eclipse
the glimmering rays of that frail virtue which Racine had depicted
as it swiftly crumbled before the close-linked temptations of erotic
love and autocratic power. The time is ripe for both to be given
wider scope: and this development is precisely what Lohenstein
proceeds to show in the course of his two plays. It is a token of his
originality and a measure of his psychological and broader cultural
vision that he selects what he considered to be the four cardinal
features of this complex process and exploits them in deft per-
mutation to generate the plots and outcomes of his two chrono-
logically consecutive and intimately interconnected plays. Both
chart the triumphant rise of the 'glorious whore' Poppaea and the
corresponding fall of the 'sententious gown-man' Seneca, and each
concentrates on the confrontation between Nero and one of his
chief adversaries, and his ultimate triumph over both of them.

His first adversary is his mother Agrippina. Imperious and

immoral, like her son, she is determined to maintain her hold on him and his affections by all means fair or foul. His historically documented attempt to rid himself of this maternal burden by causing her pleasure-boat to sink at sea is counterbalanced by her equally authenticated attempt to reverse the course of nature by seducing him, an event which Lohenstein makes all the more salacious by his oblique way of presenting it. On the face of it, the form is quite conventional: he simply uses the techniques in those days generally prescribed for handling episodes which cannot be shown on stage. But in this case the narration of the outrage is entrusted to the concubine whom Poppaea has supplanted in Nero's bed. And what better audience for an unashamed account of what took place than the stoic philosopher Seneca, Nero's moral tutor, and Burrhus, the loyally devoted prefect of his bodyguard? The inherent virtue of her listeners makes her exaggerate the sordid details of the seduction out of perverse delight in shocking them: she is fighting a losing battle with her rivals Poppaea and now Agrippina too, and all is fair in love and politics. Meanwhile her wider audience, the audience beyond the footlights, is in increasing danger of losing its own moral bearings as in all these high-baroque erotic dramas. The felicities of metaphorical language no longer correspond to accepted moral values.

The dowager Empress Agrippina is one of Nero's two main adversaries, and hers is the pitiless struggle of like to vanquish like: a vain attempt to hold her own against the rising fortunes of her younger rival, Poppaea. The situation is one which was repeated time and again in high-baroque drama and in the Italian *opera seria* so closely related to it and which was to outlive it on the stages of most European countries. His other adversary is a woman too, a former slave called Epicharis. But here the struggle is a different one: two ways of being and behaving are diametrically opposed. The steps this idealistic patriot takes against the tyrant come to nothing: her plot is foiled. One by one, she and her fellow conspirators are unmasked and dragged to death in Nero's torture chambers, or ordered to remove themselves in the traditional Roman manner by committing suicide, like Seneca himself. The Empress and slave are defeated and, as in Monteverdi's opera, tyrant and mistress are shown to triumph over every obstacle. Yet Lohenstein's two dramatic masterpieces, if taken together as they should be, form a work of baroque art as consistent with itself as

Monteverdi's; a work of art which in its dynamic range and spatial sense leaves questions of moral justice and poetic beauty far behind, in its pursuit of an ideal more characteristic of its age. Far more, even, than *Britannicus*, that favourite of the French classical stage, Lohenstein's 'Roman' tragedies reveal the basic fact that the baroque is what all classicism most abhors, and none more so than the pseudo-Grecian neoclassicism of static balance and patent moral purpose which came to dominate the post-baroque period in eighteenth-century Europe.

In Lohenstein what prevails is the unpredictability of life. Yet whatever the contortions of the action, the basic designs and patterns of existence are there supporting it in their essential and eternal way. But they are not evident to the naked and astonished eye, dazzled as it is by all the swirling imagery, the gilt and ornamentation. The playwright, however, and the architect, they know otherwise. For all the immediate and superficial wonder such art arouses, the greatest wonder is that, underneath its surface, there are supporting shapes and structures as brave and simple in their way as those that underlie man and his universe — or so at least claimed Galileo, Leeuwenhoek and Newton. The great men of contemporary science looked at heaven and at man beneath it through their optic glasses; the telescope made distance fall away, while under the microscope even the invisible loomed large. And while the scientists of the seventeenth century were scrutinizing stars and human sperm with implications of the most far-reaching kind, their colleagues in the spheres of art and letters were doing something similar in their way. Discarding, at their bravest, moral scruples and traditional views of beauty, truth and goodness, they were directing their inquisitive attention at human motivations and responses within the context of historical fact or long-established myth. Hence the overwhelming interest shown in situations so familiar and so frequently repeated in painting and on the stage that in retrospect we find it hard to realize that, far from being boring, they never failed to arouse curiosity and wonder. Hence, too, the zest for certain key figures such as Poppaea, Seneca and Nero. Great souls are capable of the worst vices and the finest virtues, said Descartes. Their complex interaction has never been so bravely drawn in European literature since.

Of Racine and Corneille it has frequently been said that they abandoned the traditional sphere of drama — action — to concentrate on the subtler sphere of underlying motivation. They did so in accordance with the growing taste in cultivated circles throughout Europe for the analysis of human passions, if not always for introspection. An age which attached such great importance to etiquette and manners, and generally preferred gregarious life at court or in society to isolation — best left to scholars, misanthropes and mystics — was naturally disposed to enjoy the refinements of endless debate about the rival claims of different emotions and passions both in the pastoral world of swains and shepherdesses and in the corridors of courts and palaces. However artificial such interests may seem, they really did reflect current realities. Even the conspiracy which Lohenstein dramatized in *Epicharis*, and which involved a conflict between opposing conceptions of social and political action, anticipated with extraordinary acumen the scares that ran through high society in various parts of Europe in the 1670s — associated in particular with the murky *affaire des poisons* in France, incriminating even Madame de Montespan, and with the trumped-up 'Popish Plot' in England, with its rumours of attempts on the king's life. The sinister machinations associated with the suspects in these shady doings seemed all too credible to the avid theatregoers of the period and to the readers of its baroque novels. When far more importance was attached to common issues than to individual problems, and all things tended to be seen as parts of greater wholes, it is no wonder that in reality, too, imaginations could run riot.

Exceptions to the rules of general behaviour, and rejections of the norms such codes implied, could be viewed either as grandly tragic or, in lighter vein, as laughably preposterous. Alceste in love and seeking solitude by passionately rejecting the shallow world around him could figure as the protagonist of a comedy, *Le Misanthrope* (1666), despite the poignant implications of his personal and social plight to modern audiences no longer attuned to the priorities and criteria of Molière's age. And the tendency to give and take in final formal marriage, foisted even on Cordelia by Nahum Tate in his baroque adaptation of *King Lear* in 1680, was a reflection of that wider pattern which by and large prevailed from the moment when Louis XIV 'removed the Pyrenees' by taking Marie-Thérèse to wife. Within the year he made Louise de la Vallière his royal mistress: making the best of both worlds was a philosophy much favoured throughout the period, to gild the lily seemed a noble aim, and life, at best, was but a comedy, as everybody knew.

Molière could hold his own in such a world, but he did so in the kind of play which now no longer figures in the accepted canon which later taste and literary criticism were to label 'classical'. As his contribution to the entertainments which took place on the 'enchanted isle' in 1664, he produced a *comédie galante* interspersed with musical and choreographic numbers entitled *La Princesse d'Élide*. It turns on the practical lesson which a chaste and frigid princess has to learn: 'vivre sans aimer n'est pas proprement vivre'. Can this exemplary devotee of cold Diana be taught the language of voluptuous Venus? It takes a handsome and gallant young prince to bring about the obvious dénouement, a prince who has already recognized those fundamental tenets of the baroque ethos, namely that love is a recognition of spiritual beauty,

> Et qu'il est malaisé que, sans être amoureux,
> Un jeune prince soit et grand et généreux.

Love is the gateway to more heroic virtues; but, this being a comedy, even princes can resort to subterfuge in order to gain their objective. Prince Euryale adopts the same frigid attitude as the princess, affects the same disdain for love, and thereby prompts her to embrace the norm she had rejected. Disdain for love may be her proudest virtue, but what is a virtue in a woman is in a man a crime; such coldness suggests an unacceptably low regard for feminine beauty, and deprives her of the tribute that is her traditional and eternal due. The princess is compelled by Euryale's attitude to fight with other weapons; hers was Diana's soul cast in the flesh of Venus, but now Venus has won her, heart and soul, although she doesn't know it. The interplay of jealousy and rejection, and the ploys of erotic love controlled by a due regard for polite conduct, lead to the only sort of final climax which could satisfy an audience on an enchanted island: a pastoral chorus sings the joys of love acknowledged and reciprocated, while all admire the heroine's change of heart proclaimed by the goddess Venus.

Love is the force which motivates our noblest actions; this view is expressed in Molière's comedy and in a thousand other products of the amorous baroque muse. Sometimes, as in the pastoral world of *Il Pastor Fido* and *L'Astrée*, love refines our souls. More often, such sentiments are used to bring about the consummation to be wished. For baroque love, like politics, speaks words so fair that, paradoxically, they can sometimes actually imply the cruder meanings concealed beneath their flowery, high-flown surface. 'Aux plus nobles actions elle pousse les coeurs', says Molière in an elegant alexandrine which might equally well have been written by Pierre Corneille or his fashionable brother Thomas, or by Quinault, who wrote the texts for Lully's operas. But its erotic potential is at once revealed by the aristocratic rake, John Wilmot, Earl of Rochester. In poems like *The Imperfect Enjoyment* he brings home the amorous obligations imposed by the baroque erotic ethos:

> My flutt'ring soul, sprung with the pointed kiss,
> Hangs hov'ring o're her balmy limbs of bliss.
> But whilst her busy hand wou'd guide that part,
> Which shou'd convey my soul up to her heart,
> In liquid raptures I dissolve all o're,
> Melt into sperm and spend at every poor.

The effect may be repulsive, lewd to the point of banal frankness, or so contrived as to ring untrue. Yet even lines such as these bring home the remarkable extent to which the artificial language of the baroque was able to express the very real tensions and paradoxes which seventeenth-century man — and not just he — felt when brought face to face with a phenomenon such as love. Love was seen as the point at which the senses and the spirit meet: an encounter whose enormous range and impact could be successfully expressed by baroque poets and artists thanks to their awareness of the fundamental distinction between the sensuous pleasures of love-making in itself and those, more permanent and public, of language, form and colour.

To use fair words to dress up foul motives is the prerogative of bombastic tyrants. But even heroes have their rhetorical lapses, especially when in love like Alexander the Great in Nathaniel Lee's most popular play, *The Rival Queens*, produced at Drury Lane in 1677 and still performed well into the nineteenth century. The closeness of the erotic issues in this high-flown melodrama with those expressed more intimately by Rochester becomes clear in the amorous encounter between the hero, Alexander, and Statira, his second queen, at the climax of Act III:

> *Statira*   My dearest, my all love, my lord, my king,
> You shall not die, if that the soul and body
> Of thy Statira can restore thy life.

> Give me thy wonted kindness, bend me, break me
> With thy embraces.
> *Alexander*   O, the killing joy!
> O, ecstasy! My heart will burst my breast
> To leap into thy bosom. . .
> So swell thy lips, so fill me with thy sweetness,
> Thou shalt not sleep, nor close thy wand'ring eyes.
> The smiling hours shall all be loved away,
> We'll surfeit all the night, and languish all the day.

Are such words in keeping with a famous royal hero? Or are they
really those of a Restoration rake, like Rochester, about to take a
tumble with his mistress? Or both? King Charles II was a consummate prince, astute and cultivated, but equally well known for his
erotic ardours; and his love for his best-remembered mistress, the
actress Nell Gwynn, began when he heard her speak the epilogue to
Dryden's *Tyrannic Love* (1669). Love was indeed the tyrant then;
and the power of beauty, wit and rhetoric captured a reigning king.
Or was it all the other way around? Statira's earlier description of
Alexander puts into words the effect that every European courtier
and man of the world hoped to achieve, words that emphasize the
practical results of the period's stress on the art of eloquent
speaking and on fulsome courtesy:

> Then he will talk, good gods, how he will talk!
> Even when the joy he sighed for is possessed,
> He speaks the kindest words and looks such things,
> Vows with such passion, swears with so much grace,
> That 'tis a kind of heaven to be deluded by him.

But the disenchantment that almost inevitably results from a surfeit
of such elegant overblown passion is then in its turn expressed by
Alexander's first wife, Roxana, speaking on behalf of all the
contemporary women who found themselves the victims of the
baroque erotic ethos, cast-off, deceived, supplanted. She too has
heard the hero's honeyed words and been deluded by their poetry:

> Gods! That a man should be so great and base!
> What said he not, when in the bridal bed
> He clasped my yielding body in his arms,
> When, with his fiery lips devouring mine,

And holding with his hand my throbbing breast,
He swore the globes of heav'n and earth were vile
To those rich worlds; and talked, and kissed, and loved,
And made me shame the morning with my blushes.

In one of his essays Sir Francis Bacon had observed that 'The speaking in a perpetual hyperbole is common in nothing but love.' But what had been a characteristic mannerism associated with Elizabethan and Jacobean lovers or, more bombastically, with tyrants cast in the Senecan mould, like Marlowe's Tamburlaine, began during the seventeenth century to invade every sphere of literary and cultured speech in all the languages of civilized Europe. Chaste eloquence became confused with voluptuous grandiloquence; there was, it seemed, no beauty any more except in exaggeration. Such was the outcome of the increasing emphasis on playing social roles and on the notion that self-advancement is most readily procured through deft employment of the art of speaking. This art had long been prized in both the pulpit and the lawcourt, and during the Renaissance it became admired in refined and courtly circles too; in other words, it flourished in the three main spheres of activity which in times of peace were open to men of breeding and education. Verbal dexterity was universally valued as an indication of a man's intelligence and presence of mind, and to be articulate in the type of language currently in fashion was widely regarded as a passport to success. To this end young men were trained in grammar schools, academies and colleges in every part of Europe; whatever the denominational differences, all agreed that eloquence was an accomplishment as valuable as fencing, dancing, horsemanship and music-making. It clearly also served the higher aims of true religion, so that it could be said that in the baroque world eloquence came next to godliness. But it was in the secular domain that it was most important, for here it served the aim of social intercourse. The pursuits and interests of men and women were quite distinct in the seventeenth century, as indeed they have been in every cultural age before our own. In post-Renaissance Europe lovemaking was the only opportunity to overcome this traditional segregation, and the language of love became a baroque *lingua franca*. Both sexes could display wit and ingenuity in this domain to mutual advantage; indeed the emergence of love as the central topic of conversation in polite society was as much the

ladies' doing as the men's. Only in this one sphere could women
and men demonstrate that they were equals, and only here could
women show that they too had an essential social and cultural role
to play. In many respects the resultant situation in the courts and
salons of seventeenth-century Europe was reminiscent of the secular
culture of the high Middle Ages, with its cults of chivalry and
courtly love. Indeed the fourteenth-century Italian poet Petrarch,
the great exponent of the sonnet form, provides a link between
these two widely separated eras; he drew on his own rich medieval
background of selfless love and amorous devotion to create the
potent literary language of Renaissance and baroque love poetry
enshrined in the Petrarchan sonnet and the style and imagery
associated with it. In Renaissance Italy and then gradually in other
parts of Europe too, a woman could achieve as idealized loved one
or as inspiring lover a degree of independent social standing which
eluded her in her other more conventional roles as daughter, wife
and mother, the roles allotted her in Christian Europe. No doubt
this was one of the most cogent reasons why so many of the famous
and successful women of baroque Europe chose to emulate the
example of literature and occupy the precarious but often rewarding position of mistress to men of standing and distinction.
From the moment in 1684 when Madame de Maintenon decided to
break with this tradition and become the morganatic, unofficial
wife of Louis XIV instead of his official mistress, the erosion of
baroque values had begun.

The world in which such opportunities could open up was a
privileged and small one: this should not be forgotten. It was
restricted almost entirely to court and aristocratic circles, and scope
for secular success was therefore limited in the extreme. Fortunate
indeed, in baroque eyes, were the galaxy of beauties who actually
succeeded in captivating princes and kings. Few women managed
to live out the ideal so frequently upheld, and to become modern
Poppaeas and Statiras: Madame de Montespan, the Duchesses of
Richmond, Cleveland and Portsmouth — these are among the few
that have remained in the memory: antiquity had more to show
than that! As for the rest, those forgotten beauties whose likenesses
hang by the dozen in the palaces and country houses of baroque
Europe: there is a lack of individuality about them, just as there is
about the nymphs whose cruel charms were sung in countless
well-turned lyrics. Now and again, one's attention is arrested by a

line or image in a love poem by Hofmann von Hofmannswaldau or
Sir Charles Sedley, or by a glance, a feature caught in a portrait by
Sir Peter Lely or Sir Godfrey Kneller: a spark of life flares up amidst
the habitual languor of high-born ladies playing conventional parts
and immortalized in stereotyped poses. But in general these gilt-
framed ladies are the visual embodiments, paint, jewels and all, of
their innumerable poetic counterparts. Names like Phyllis, Chloris,
Celimena, Flavia and, above all, heavenly Celia, evoke the glamour
of a vanished age when, for the privileged few, art and sex were
intimately fused. But even this exclusive glamour could sometimes
pall, as the Earl of Dorset realized:

> Methinks the Poor Town has been troubled too long
> With *Phillis* and *Cloris* in every Song;
> By fools, who at once can both love and despair,
> And will never leave calling them cruel and fair.

The town he had in mind was of course London; but the same held
true of every other major European city.

Their lovers, too, could sometimes wish with Alexander the
Great that there were other worlds to conquer. Hyperbole or not,
the sentiment had much to recommend it especially to the speaker
on this occasion — none other than Don Juan in Molière's version
of the well-known subject, *Dom Juan* (1665). None of his great
comedies so fully reveals his major stature as a baroque writer. To
his already teeming gallery of seventeenth-century types and figures
he now added that of the aristocratic rake or libertine at his most
persuasive and complete. Just like Nero or the despotic emperor
Maximin in *Tyrannic Love*, Don Juan and all his counterparts in life
and literature can plead as his excuse:

> If to new persons I my love apply,
> The stars and nature are at fault, not I.

Indeed in Thomas Shadwell's adaptation of the legend to suit the
taste of Restoration London (*The Libertine*, 1675), the Don actually
paraphrases Dryden's heroic couplet in casual prose worthy of Lord
Rochester: 'Let's on and live the noble life of sense: if we be bad,
'tis Nature's fault that made us so.' Don Juan's remark pinpoints
the central theme of the libertine outlook which surfaced in various
parts of Europe during the high-baroque period. Its emergence was
closely linked to the changing attitudes towards education and

social behaviour already outlined, and it caught on especially with some of the products of that system when they encountered the adult world at court, rather than in the church or lawcourts.

Like neostoicism, which had been the guiding philosophical system of the early baroque period, libertine thinking had origins which lay far back in classical antiquity. But it was to very different areas of ancient philosophy that it turned in its attempts to provide a viable outlook which would help the individual to meet and overcome the perils and challenges of the baroque world; not stoicism this time, that stern rejection of the sensual, but epicureanism instead, with its glad acceptance of material things. Just as the Flemish thinker Lipsius had represented the revival of stoic attitudes in alliance with the doctrines of the church — a powerful combination in times of religious unrest and renewal — so now, in the high-baroque period, another contemporary thinker must take much of the credit for the new intellectual departure. In 1649 the French mathematician Pierre Gassendi published a Latin guide to the Greek philosopher Epicurus and his ideas. The time was opportune; soon his book, *Philosophiae Epicuri Syntagma*, became the theoretical basis and intellectual justification at first or second hand for a new approach to life and living. Once again an ancient philosophy (one of affirmation this time, not of abnegation) was being revitalized, and once again this was happening in conjunction with a momentous new phenomenon: the rise of mathematics and scientific method. To thinking men in the high-baroque period this combination seemed even more persuasive than that of Christianity and stoicism because it encouraged and justified their aims and requirements. The tense mid-century period of unrest was coming to an end, and the return of stability and general peace enhanced the appeal of a philosophy which upheld human happiness as a principle and regarded peace of mind, not stoic apathy, as the supreme good for which all men should strive.

A life-enhancing philosophy, and one which actively enjoined the exploration of the material world, not its rejection or transcendence, had much to recommend it to the dissolute young noblemen who returned from cavalier exile in France and Holland with Charles II in 1660. They rejected the impediments of tradition and authority and scorned, in private, the moral teachings of the church; in their eyes natural morality went hand in hand with natural science, pursuit of pleasure with scientific inquiry. It was therefore to be expected that a great many of the men of leisure who devoted their time and wealth to amateur research and scientific pastimes were advocates of this new trend of thought. Soon the formal institutions of the rising intellectual movement were being set up in different parts of Europe. The Accademia del Cimento ('Academy of Experiments') in Florence was brilliant but shortlived (1657-67). In Paris, Colbert, controller of the royal finances, established the equally illustrious but longer-lasting Académie Royale des Sciences under Louis XIV's patronage in 1666, with a membership that included most of the distinguished intellectual names in Europe. Slightly ahead of this, Charles II and his gifted Anglo-German cousin, Prince Rupert of the Rhine, were enrolled as active members of the Royal Society for Improving Human Knowledge (1662), thus clearly demonstrating the significant fact that interests of this kind were compatible with the baroque concept of society and as much a part of the baroque way of life as gallant talk and amorous flirtation.

Little of the work of Epicurus had survived from ancient times. But many of his ideas had been taken up by the Roman philosopher-poet Lucretius and were available in print for all to read. His enormous scientific epic poem *De rerum natura* is a daunting prospect, however; even to seventeenth-century readers, more used to noble diction and with more stomach for sustained argument, its intellectual demands must often have seemed extreme. But even readers lacking in persistence would probably get far enough to reach the appealing passage where Lucretius, embarking on his vast survey of materialist philosophy, addresses the Goddess Venus with the words:

> Since you alone govern the nature of all things,
> Since without you nothing sees the light of life,
> And nothing joyful or beautiful is created,
> You I entreat to help me in this undertaking.

Here indeed was an attitude in keeping with high-baroque inclinations, and it provided a perfect classical precedent for the turn which taste was taking. When Molière's Don Juan, or for that matter Shadwell's, proclaims the advantages of a 'life of sense', there is behind his words, though he may not know it, the entire weight of a comprehensive philosophical system established in Greek and Roman antiquity and taken up again in his own time.

Admittedly Don Juan's outrageous views on nature, love and freedom are righteously denounced as 'impious discourse' by the stoical hermit in Shadwell's *Libertine*: the clash between the two men, the brooding mystic and the arrogant rake, brings sharply into focus the conflict underlying the baroque period as a whole. Though brief, their argument shows us how stoicism, backed by the full weight of Christian teaching, found itself confronted by libertine materialism, embodied in a lecherous nobleman supremely sure that the intellectual future is on his side. They meet alone in the seclusion of a forest. The hermit has withdrawn from the wicked and transitory world: paradoxically this insight and his resultant action are his whole *raison d'être*. Don Juan, on the other hand, regards existence in the natural world as an end supremely enjoyable in itself. Yet the world both men inhabit is the same — the one which we call ours. Nevertheless they differ fundamentally in their conceptions of it, and their attitudes to it are irreconcilable. As if he were some devotee of a Christian Diana, the hermit has rejected Venus and all her claims, whereas the Spanish Don is ready time and again to rush into her arms, convinced of his innate ability to reconcile erotic rapture with superiority of intellect and station. We ask the question — the one which they asked then: which of these two sorts of conduct best becomes a gentleman?

The libertine outlook was open to excess and misinterpretation. Often enough, as in the notorious court circles of Restoration London, its insolently easygoing emphasis on individual freedom was little more than an excuse for self-indulgence and lecherous behaviour. Elsewhere, as in Silesia, which was at that time the literary centre of Germany, libertinism was a pose which fashionable men of letters affected, concealing beneath the deliberate lubricity of their verses a degree of personal probity which suggests that they had much less in common with their French or English counterparts than their works would have us think. The aesthetic façade of these German baroque poems is more imposing, but they lack something of the casual ease of the Restoration lyric; the worldly manner that characterizes the poetry of Sir Charles Sedley, the Earl of Rochester and their cavalier precursors like Thomas Carew or Sir John Suckling usually eludes the Germans. Instead they indulge themselves in extraordinary displays of verbal ornamentation which reach extremes of artificiality through exhausting concentration on a restricted set of stereotyped motifs. Lips of coral, rose and ruby, lily-white breasts of swan's-down or alabaster, hearts of adamant: the erotic effects created by such devices lack spontaneity and feeling. They are the products of skilled craftsmanship, finely wrought in words to have the appearance and effect of amatory ejaculations.

The masters of this cosmetic poetry of eye and cheek, hair, mouth and breast, and other delights referred to less directly, had learnt their craft in Italy, where verbal jewellery had a long tradition which went right back to Petrarch. But the Italian writer who had most appeal for them was Giambattista Marino, known as the Cavaliere Marini (1569-1625). In this brilliant Neapolitan protégé of Marie de' Medici in Paris, Hofmann von Hofmannswaldau and Lohenstein recognized the initiator of their high-baroque manner in the domain of metaphorical language, and rightly so, despite his unexpectedly early date. For Marino had indeed taken the already highly sophisticated language of Italian poetry a further step forward and away from its Renaissance perfection into new realms of stylistic artifice; and he had done this by limiting its range while at the same time making still greater provision for displays of verbal wit within these limitations. The almost classical manner of the high Renaissance — lofty themes, intense emotion, apt images and evenness of diction — gave way to imaginative flights of amorous rapture, beguilingly sensual yet so deftly handled that only a cool mind with a firm grasp of logic could write or indeed read the final graceful product. In 1623, when Marino was enjoying fame and patronage in Paris, he published his most dazzling *tour de force*, an erotic poem entitled *L'Adone*. No single poem enjoyed such reputation in baroque Europe, where it was ranked beside Guarini's pastoral drama *Il Pastor Fido* as the embodiment of verbal beauty; few works as influential have disappeared so utterly from general awareness. The literary fate of *L'Adone* is an eloquent example of the baroque theme of the transitoriness of worldly glory.

The loves of Venus and Adonis provide the theme of *L'Adone's* twenty cantos. But, like some vast and rambling baroque palace, its grandiose design is overlaid and almost destroyed by an effusiveness of detail in which contemporaries could obviously sense a unity which we no longer see. In presentation it forms a link between the late Renaissance eroticism of Shakespeare's *Venus and Adonis*

(1593), more 'marinesque' than any of his plays, and Lohenstein's triumphant paean in praise of Venus, published posthumously a full century later, in 1695. All three Venus poems have elements in common. They draw on classical sources like Ovid's *Metamorphoses*, which were favourite and influential reading in a period acutely aware of the changes and transformation to which all things are subject, and they all set out to re-create a myth to suit contemporary conventions. In doing this, they also all reflect the cultural values of their prospective readers, for popular success was very much their aim. The wit of Shakespeare's Elizabethan mini-epic, rich in conceits and allegorical imagery, reappears in more ingenious guise in the Italian epic and swells to almost incoherent richness there in order to incorporate a vision of the sensual world which would dissolve into a dreamlike muddle if it were not so cerebral, so highly wrought and coloured. Lohenstein was not aware of Shakespeare; but *L'Adone* he admired enormously. In his own German *Venus* he aspired not to outdo his model — that would have seemed unthinkable — but to compose a eulogy of the goddess of love unrivalled for its comprehensiveness. He drew on every source he could discover; making full use of his unusual fund of arcane knowledge, he brought all his gifts as a psychologically penetrating erotic poet to bear on Venus, or, rather, on the power of love not just to dominate the hearts and souls of human beings, but to animate the universe:

> Heaven, too, can feel the scorching flames of love;
> To satisfy its longing for the earth
> It gazes down at night through countless eyes. . .

This is the night sky of a universe where space itself is ruled by a god of love, and myth and scientific observation are fused to supreme effect. At her appearance in voluptuous progress through it, even this world of ours, intoxicated by her presence, transcends itself and once again becomes the perfect masterpiece it was at the Creation. No heaven as such is needed any longer; the world is a paradise, and Venus rises, glorious, to outshine the Virgin Mary.

Does Lohenstein really reject the Christian dispensation in favour of a sensual paganism? It almost seems so. At any rate his disregard for accepted moral and religious values seems even more deliberate and blatant than the carefree flouting of them by the libertine aristocrats who were his contemporaries, but who were living in a very different social setting. Their amorality was a gesture of cynical depravity or intellectual freedom; his was something significantly more. Like many of his most notable contemporaries, Germany's major high-baroque writer knew how to combine the elegant and the profound, and he could afford his probing and observant mind to range far and wide. Everything beneath the sun was open to scrutiny, not least the human mind and the emotions. God alone was exempt, and far beyond the reach of human comprehension: that austere and hidden God of Lutheranism, sublime in the oneness of His majesty, and to be attained by man through faith alone. And this is what accounts for what at first sight seems an unlikely achievement — *Venus*. The sensual world of ancient pagan myth could rise refurbished in all the rapturous splendour of baroque art precisely because it impinged so little on personal Christian faith. This, too, is why the pagan goddess of love could ride in triumph through the adoring universe endowed with many of the attributes which, in Roman Catholic countries, were reserved for the Virgin Mary. In other artists such a paean in praise of Venus might indicate a cultural crisis in any other cultural phase than the high baroque; but here there was no underlying confusion. At bottom there is far less connection between Lohenstein's cosmic vision and the glorified pornography of the libertines than there is between it and the dualism associated with the influential philosophy of Descartes. As in the paintings of Rubens or the music of Monteverdi the two spheres do not meet; each can exist and be explored in freedom.

Elsewhere, especially in Roman Catholic regions, the urge to glorify love at its most omnipotent and sublime manifested itself in other ways. The Spanish Carmelite nun, Teresa of Avila, wrote her spiritual autobiography, the *Libro de su vida* (it first appeared in 1588), and devotional treatises such as *El castillo interior* ('The inner castle') and *El camino de perfeccion* ('The way to perfection'). Hers was a commanding personality, and generated extraordinary religious zeal; her contribution to the spiritual regeneration of the church during the Counter-Reformation was unquestioned. But she was not a creative writer in the Renaissance or baroque sense; her sole intention was to record and communicate her inner experience, not to re-create it in terms of conscious art. Yet what she had to say about what she had mystically felt and seen captured the imaginations of many seventeenth-century Europeans, who realized that her life and works contained a wealth of elements awaiting exploitation. Would St Teresa have recognized herself in the ecstatic nun voluptuously awaiting the ineffable pangs and pleasure of being transfixed by the dart of a smiling angel — the likeness which Bernini created as an altarpiece for a chapel in Santa Maria della Vittoria in Rome in 1647-52? She might have found this baroque masterpiece a sham, with its heightened re-creation in aesthetic terms of a spiritual experience more real than any sculpture. Yet her humble and authentic words called out for some commensurate artistic treatment in that age which so intensely longed to fuse the eternal with the finite. Such ecstasies as hers life cannot carry long; the problem therefore is, how to preserve them? The Spanish Inquisition actually delayed the publication of her visionary writings as if it sensed the dangers they entailed, and the temptations of artistic misinterpretation or distortion. They were transcended by Bernini's genius; yet even his *Teresa* was later viewed with grave misgiving by eighteenth-century neoclassicists and Victorian critics. But there are many instances where in Bavarian or Spanish churches the spiritual effects aimed at in paint and sculpture seem spurious and shallow, where they depend too obviously on the meretricious exploitation of conventional erotic postures and motifs. Not so Bernini's statue, enhanced by its fine and formal setting:

> Thou art *Loves* Victim; and must dye
> A death more mysticall and *high*.
> Into *Loves* armes thou shalt let fall
> A still surviving funerall.
> His is the *Dart* must make the *Death*
> Whose stroake shall taste thy hallow'd *breath*;
> A Dart thrice dipt in that rich *flame*,
> Which writes thy spouses radiant *Name*,
> Upon the roofe of Heav'n

wrote Crashaw in his *Hymn to Saint Teresa* (1646). The splendours of his poem and of Bernini's sculpture are travestied in the upturned gaze, the swooning bodies and the diaphanous draperies of countless tawdry plaster visionaries.

During the years 1673-5 the visions a French nun, St Margaret Mary Alacoque, gave final shape to that supremely baroque phenomenon, the devotion of the Sacred Heart. Few products of the baroque age have survived so successfully to the present day: the visual embodiments of the cult, the statuettes and pictures, the vermilion hearts transfixed by nails and radiating rays of glittering golden light, still carry on artistic traditions established then, though in debased, conventional form. The devotion of the Sacred Heart was a development logical enough in the context of its period, an extension of the mystical and erotic possibilities inherent in the more traditional devotion of the five wounds inflicted on Christ during His Crucifixion. But now increasing attention was focused with almost obsessive fervour on one wound in particular, the wound in Christ's left side, from which transparent water, symbolizing baptism, and the scarlet blood of the Eucharist flowed. Behind and deep within His holy body, but revealing itself in ever-swelling fullness to worshippers in intense adoration like St Margaret Mary, behind the abused flesh of the divine and dying Jesus, the source of these symbolic fluids glowed in crimson glory — that Heart whose unfathomable capacity for loving embraced mankind and bled for its redemption. A potent symbol for the reciprocal love between man and his God had been discovered, and it became an integral part of baroque art and religious attitudes even in Protestant countries. From the start, it blended with more secular factors: with pagan motifs such as Cupid's arrow, with elements of biblical symbolism like the spouse and bride of the Song of Solomon, and with the figurative devices of Petrarchan love poetry, itself inherited from the Middle Ages and their courtly love and mystical devotion. As a result, the visual details of the Christian cult, like the mystical language associated with it, are often almost interchangeable with those of more secular and overtly erotic contexts. Each European language found in its resources appropriate elements which could be exploited to excellent advantage; indeed the presence in individual languages of certain ready-made associations (such as the *Herz—Schmerz* rhyme in German) led some people to the supernatural conclusion that there was a pre-existent mystical signification inherent in language itself.

In religious art and poetry the straining after high-flown expression, far-fetched similes and histrionic gestures could lead to a distortion of genuine mystical experience and to a degradation of spiritual love as blatant and superficial in its way as the trivialization of love on a more earthly level manifest in most libertine verse. The intrinsically secular figure of Don Juan, whose licentious

presence haunts the literature and culture of baroque Europe, has
its spiritual counterparts, like Molière's Tartuffe, self-seekers always
in search of meretricious experiences and visions, and ready to enjoy
delicious anticipations of heaven while still on earth; impostors
never at a loss for apt and honeyed words in which to hide their
motives. And, closely associated with them, there is St Mary
Magdalene, that favourite figure of all baroque Europe; the fallen
woman whose sins, that were many, were all forgiven because she
loved much, as Our Lord had said. In her, seventeenth-century men
beheld the victim of their innumerable seductions raised to a
celestial beauty; in her weeping penitence she appeared more
seductive than she was before, and radiated a deep fascination
which they captured in many a religious painting and poem, in
English the finest surely being Crashaw's exuberantly Italianate
effusion, *The Weeper*:

> O pretious prodigall!
> Faire spend-thrift of thy self! Thy measure
> (Mercilesse love!) is all,
> Even to the last pearl in thy treasure:
> All places, times, and objects be,
> Thy teares sweet opportunity.

She whom angels did adore when she ceased to be a whore (thus
Hofmannswaldau in an epigram!) had become a vital baroque
symbol of the interplay and ultimate fusion of sexuality and
spiritual yearning.

The claims and counterclaims of rival ways of loving and rival
objects of devotion take up much of any seventeenth-century work
dealing with love; whether in a sonnet in the Petrarchan manner or
a pastoral novel in the manner of *L'Astrée*, the great debate went
on with unabated zest until the rising tide of sentiment and feeling
towards the end of the century began to mark a general shift in taste
and attitude. By then the baroque was on the wane in many parts of
Europe; yet as it waned it also reached its culminating triumphs
especially in its treatment of omnipotent love. In France, Racine
portrayed the ravages of passion with classical restraint in *Phèdre*,
performed on the first day of 1677. Towards the end of that same
year Dryden produced the ripest of his dramas, *All for Love; or,
The World Well Lost*, a reworking of the story of Antony and
Cleopatra whose very title conveys a baroque readiness to abandon

all considerations of morality and political expediency for the sake of rapturous love.

> See Europe, Afric, Asia put in balance,
> And all weighed down by one light, worthless woman!

exclaims the stalwart officer Ventidius in reply to Antony's doting caution:

> No word of Cleopatra; she deserves
> More worlds than I can lose.

The ironic echo of Alexander's vain request for other worlds to conquer cannot conceal the fact that for Antony, as for all men, there is only one to lose — the world he lives in. But to die in losing it or lose it dying is the supreme vindication of baroque passion. Its nature and its cosmic power are embodied in Cleopatra, the fair Egyptian queen; and Ventidius, the Roman looker-on, is made the mouthpiece for some of Dryden's most haunting insights, paintings in words that surely have no equals in all the painted treatments of this subject:

> She's dangerous:
> Her eyes have power beyond Thessalian charms,
> To draw the moon from heaven; for eloquence,
> The sea-green Syrens taught her voice their flattery;
> And, while she speaks, night steals upon the day,
> Unmarked by those that hear: then she's so charming,
> Age buds at sight of her, and swells to youth:
> The holy priests gaze on her when she smiles;
> And with heaved hands, forgetting gravity,
> They bless her wanton eyes: even I who hate her,
> With a malignant joy behold such beauty;
> And, while I curse, desire it.

The allusions here to the perils of love; the charms of eye and voice; to the sea, birthplace of Venus and symbolical of the mysteries of life; to age and youth, here with their roles reversed in an appropriately chosen conceit with just a touch of erotic *double entendre*: all these are baroque elements and culminate in a picture of the queen which makes her look like Mary Magdalene, and so prepares us for the final paradox, so typical of the Petrarchan manner, of love and hate in simultaneous fusion. Ventidius's picture is baroque in every telling detail.

The goddess Venus? Or just some city harlot charming the senses of a lubric and adulterate age? There is a common similarity about the baroque age's embodiments of love and beauty like there is between the portraits of its most admired women or the protestations of undying devotion that occur in its plays and novels. It is therefore revealing to discover which mythical lovers or historical love stories it most admired and delighted in. There are, for instance, no Romeos and Juliets among them; it had scant sympathy for the tragedy of youthful passion, although it did appreciate the amorous eloquence of Shakespeare's lovers. Nor did it have much interest in the strains and stresses of love the victim of social class and economic status; that became a burning topic later, during the second half of the eighteenth century, as did the sentimental pathos inherent in romantic disregard for social distinctions in the name of a shared humanity. 'La personne et le rang ne se séparent point', declares the heroine of one of Corneille's later 'Roman' plays. Her statement provides an essential key to baroque social attitudes. And they in turn affected art and literature deeply; the period's favourite subjects make this very clear.

Certain basic amorous situations recur throughout the literature of the period, and it is clearly significant that they are often found in art and music too. Generally they are associated with a pair of famous lovers: Antony and Cleopatra, Sophonisba and Massinissa, Titus and Berenice are the endlessly enthralling subjects of operas and paintings, some famous, others long forgotten, as too are Dido, the Carthaginian queen, and her Trojan lover Aeneas, from Virgil's *Aeneid*. There may also be deep cultural significance in the fact that each of these representative baroque subjects illustrates a momentous encounter between the ordered European world of ancient Rome and other ways of life beyond its confines, where priorities are different and other values are upheld. In each of these tales of deep and searing conflict, divergent loyalties and obligations are brought out as the result of love, whose sway is elemental and universal. For seventeenth-century Europeans the struggle between the claims of love and duty, whether political, erotic or spiritual, or all together, was the most immediate way of clarifying their own ideals and attitudes. They loved to see this struggle represented on the stage or captured in the shapes and colours of painting, the tonalities and rhythms of music.

No wonder Sophonisba topped the bill! The flare-up of sexual passion against an exotic background of North African warfare; this was as congenial to the Venetian opera-house as to the London or Paris stage. Sophonisba, a Carthaginian queen like Dido, is taken prisoner by Massinissa, a hot-blooded African prince; but being Rome's ally, he is compelled to hand her over. Unable to possess all that he most desires, he kills her out of love, and she, in dying, acknowledges its final victory. This was the moment Rembrandt, along with many other baroque painters, chose to paint. It was a subject that had exerted some appeal during the Renaissance. But not until the high baroque did it begin to challenge the creative ingenuity of major artists. Pierre Corneille produced a version in 1663; soon he was followed by Lohenstein (1669) and by Nathaniel Lee (1676). Central for all of them is the climactic moment when Scipio, embodying the cold morality of republican Rome, commands his tributary, Massinissa, to renounce his love and hand Sophonisba over to her Roman victors. He cannot, yet he must; and his response provides the opportunity to proclaim the claims of love in true heroic manner. Lee, for example, handles the episode with a characteristic blend of hyperbole and passion. In answer to Scipio's stern advice, 'her memory forget!', the prince retorts:

> Cut me to Atoms, tear my Soul out; yet
> In every smallest particle of me
> You shall the Form of *Sophonisba* see:
> All like my Soul, and all in ev'ry part;
> Bath'd in my Eyes, and bleeding in my Heart!

Epicurean and Platonist philosophy and scientific atomism are aptly drawn upon to justify his attitude; but equally telling is the way they merge into a conceit, quasi-religious yet ardently erotic, and worthy of the Italian Marino.

Love in high conflict with the claims and duties of high station: this is the central theme of Titus and Berenice. In November 1670 plays on this subject by Corneille and Racine were first performed almost simultaneously in Paris. Racine's brought tears to the eyes of an audience starting to tire of passions and heroics; intimacy and pathos, these Racine provided in chaste and classical form. Pruned of grandiloquence and relying on simpler beauties for its effect, it was a move towards an anti-baroque neoclassicism equivalent to the rejection of Cavalli's opera and Bernini's grand designs for the Louvre; a prelude to the taste of eighteenth-century Europe which

France was to dominate. It also meant a setback for Corneille. No longer quite the darling of poetic fashion, his *Tite et Bérénice* was another splendid example of that personal brand of the baroque which makes him one of its greatest exponents in his declining years. A 'heroic comedy' he called it, as if to suggest that in his baroque view the outcome vindicates the sacrifice and proves that noble action is indeed a worthy and happy end. The atmosphere is extravagantly polite; echoes of ancient Rome blend imperceptibly with the heroic ethos of a modern age which, in France at least, was by now already waning. It is a world where even the crudest lusts and most intimate feelings appear in the resplendent guise of noble sentiment and high-sounding diction. But is it really such a hollow world? This late Cornelian Rome, where the flames of love and the gleam of diadems seem to be the sole concern of all involved, is certainly a complete antithesis of modern realism. Yet the world Corneille and his contemporaries lived in had its full share of cruelty and hardship. The gibbet stood at every roadside, while the pox both great and small took its toll and disfigured the appearance of those lucky enough to survive the perils of birth and infancy; rank, duty and ambition then saw to it that sacrifices were demanded of them which we would consider inhuman. And nowhere was this more so than in the domain of love renounced and of enforced marriage. Is the world of *Tite et Bérénice* an escape from such harsh realities? Or is it an audacious attempt to look them in the face and challenge them to take on sufficient meaning to justify the sufferings inflicted in their name?

The aim of Corneille's baroque art is to beautify the passions, to make us admire our fellow men and women and realize the potential in ourselves. Domitie, a high-born Roman woman, is ready to renounce her inclinations by marrying Titus, her emperor: but he is now in love with Berenice, a beautiful foreigner, and may defy convention and tradition by marrying her instead. It now becomes as imperative for Domitie to prevent this marriage happening as it is for her lover, Domitian, to encourage it for his own sake to win her back. All the ingredients are present on which European opera was to go on drawing for another hundred years or more, and which was to reach its culmination in the sequence of late baroque music dramas which Handel wrote for London between 1711 and 1741 (*Berenice*, 1737). Ridiculously contrived yet deeply felt, their world has much in common with the passionate heroics of the semi-tragic plays Corneille had written more than half a century before. In both, the threat of boredom looms as we are treated to a chain of stilted sentiments and emotions; then suddenly a vision opens, a line rings true, a melody delights us, and we are faced with greatness.

Greatness and its cognate quality, grandeur, the baroque age prized probably above all else, yet they could prove elusive. The story of Dido and Aeneas certainly ensured continuing popularity for Virgil's epic in the seventeenth century. Other periods may have preferred other features of the poem; but when Virgil took his Trojan hero from burning Troy to sumptuous Carthage and showed him so enamoured of Queen Dido that his heroic purpose faltered and the future destiny of Rome hung in the balance, he had created a myth close to the heart and spirit of baroque Europe. The issues were congenial. Love and ambition, duty and inclination in conflict against a backcloth of heroic adventure and exotic colour: all this was immediately accessible to modern readers, and the story found its way into baroque poetry and painting as a potent and familiar allusion. Yet only once did it really come to life again throughout the baroque period in Europe. Even Cavalli's opera *La Didone* pales before the unique splendours of *Dido and Aeneas*, the opera which Henry Purcell wrote for performance by a Chelsea girls' school in 1689. It is extraordinarily compact. Purcell achieves his heightening of heroic situations and emotions with none of the bombast and inflation that was so much admired in his day. Yet in a good production his masterpiece can convey a quintessence of the baroque vision of love voluptuous and tragic, and set against a background of human destiny and natural forces.

8

Life is a dream

A note of disenchantment was present in the baroque from the beginning. Its obsessive fondness for play-acting and for the metaphor of the stage reveals a deep-seated awareness that appearances are illusion, while its philosophical basis in Christian stoicism was a constant reminder, like war, plague and fever, that life is precarious indeed in comparison to the certainty of death. 'Were the happiness of the next world as closely apprehended as the felicities of this, it were a martyrdom to live,' observed Sir Thomas Browne (1605-82). Alongside its colour and glitter and its extrovert joy of living, there is indeed a darker and more searching side to the baroque.

While the carefree masquerade of a privileged society played on in continuous counterpoint to the high drama of court life and ceremonial, there were always some among the actors and spectators who asked the question: and when the comedy is over, what then? Enormous care was taken to ensure that the obsequies of important persons were as magnificent as their stations in life warranted. The towering catafalques surrounded with a blaze of candles, the funeral processions, the requiem masses to solemn music by Cavalli, by Biber in Vienna or by Gilles and Campra in France: these were ephemeral pomps whose memory is almost forgotten. But even the monuments designed and carved by the greatest sculptors — Bernini's tombs for Pope Urban VIII and Pope Alexander VII, for instance, or their imitations by Roubiliac and Rysbrack in Westminster Abbey — were conceived and viewed with oddly mixed feelings. On the one hand they were of course meant to perpetuate the memory and fame of the defunct: indeed they had a double function, as monuments and as works of art, to challenge and outlive the oblivion of eternity. Yet at the same time, as everyone knew, pyramids, arches, obelisks, what were they but the irregularities of vainglory, wild enormities erected in futile defiance of the inevitable, no more lasting than pillars of snow? All over Europe thoughtful people shared the view expressed with rare perfection by Browne in the meditation on death and transience which he called by the curiously erudite title *Hydriotaphia, or Urn-Burial* (1658):

> In vain do individuals hope for immortality, or any patent from oblivion, in preservations below the moon: men have been deceived even in their flatteries above the sun, and studied conceits to perpetuate their names in heaven. While we look for incorruption in the heavens, we find they are but like the earth; durable in their main bodies, alterable in their parts: whereof, beside comets and new stars, perspectives begin to tell tales, and the spots that wander about the sun, with Phaeton's favour, would make clear conviction. There is nothing strictly immortal but immortality; whatever hath no beginning may be confident of no end. . .

Sun spots had been observed by Galileo and simultaneously by Kepler in the early years of the seventeenth century. In 1600 the German astronomer had arrived in Prague, the seat of the eccentric Holy Roman Emperor Rudolf II: a strange, remote world where Spanish cultural influences (the emperor had been brought up in Habsburg Spain) mingled with those of Italy, post-Reformation Germany and Counter-Reformation Austria on territory which was essentially Slav. There, in this microcosm of our labyrinth of a world, the Imperial Mathematician Kepler gazed heavenward and made his calculations, constantly striving to penetrate the mysteries of the universe and comprehend the harmonies he knew must underlie its structure. The complicated geometrical diagrams that illustrate his observations of the cosmos which Copernicus had already partially revealed look out from the printed pages of his learned publications like groundplans and sections for baroque cathedrals. The shapes-within-shapes, the multiple spheres and polyhedrons all balanced in intricate mathematical relation to each other: all reveal his conception of a cosmos which really does make

sense despite the apparent irregularity of its details to ignorant eyes.
But the sense it makes is on a scale so vast that it quite transcends
the dimensions of this world and opens up unimagined perspectives. Scientific visions such as Kepler's point to a transcendent
meaning which makes a mockery of earthbound thinking; yet they
seem as artificial as baroque art and music. But then all things are
by definition artificial to those like Kepler who regard nature as the
art of God.

In 1619 the young Descartes, eager to read the book of the world
open all around him, was returning from the Netherlands to
France. On the road an almost mystical experience overwhelmed
him: he realized that the material universe makes sense. Descartes's
conviction that the world can be understood by means of mathematics and logical thinking was to have profound effects on
intellectual and scientific progress. In gratitude for the revelation
that had been vouchsafed him, he vowed to make a pilgrimage to
one of baroque Europe's favourite holy places, the shrine of the
Holy House at Loreto, which pious legend says was transplanted
there from Nazareth through the miraculous agency of angels. But
there was no paradox in this conduct, not yet, not even to
Descartes's thinking. Like the Frenchman's vision of the boundless
possibilities of scientific method when rationally applied by well-
trained minds, the laws of planetary motion enunciated by the
German Kepler in his *New Astronomy* (1609) and *Harmonice
Mundi* ('Harmony of the World') of 1619 may not have exerted any
immediate or direct influence on the course art and literature were
taking; even in those days of broad-based scholarship it was not
always easy to harmonize the spheres of science and aesthetics. Yet
Kepler's emphasis on elliptical motion and on the observation that
the heavenly bodies can form constant patterns despite the fact that
they cannot be static has many obvious elements in common with
the restless movement and the formalism of baroque art. The
presence of similar underlying concepts in the music of the
period — a constant ground-bass in counterpoint with melodic
lines and florid ornamentation, for instance; the 'regularity' respected by even its most experimental poets; the emphasis on proportion and perspective evident even in its most ebullient paintings:
all these are pointers in the same direction. And it was this
recognition of fundamental laws and transcendental order which
made it possible for this fragile life of ours, this vale of tears, to be

dismissed as mere illusion without the inevitable disenchantment ever actually leading to what might otherwise have been its logical sequel: black despair. No major figure of the baroque age committed suicide — except the Roman architect Borromini, and that was probably the result of mental sickness.

> A man that looks on glasse
> On it may stay his eye;
> Or if he pleaseth, through it passe,
> And then the heav'n espie.

The familiar lines of George Herbert's poem 'The Elixier' (from *The Temple*, 1633) are a characteristic expression of the baroque consciousness of the coexistence of two almost entirely distinct planes of vision. The worldly and the celestial, the material and the spiritual, the transitory and the eternal: there are many ways of describing them, just as there were many ways of using glass as a commodity or as a symbol. To people in seventeenth-century Europe, glass had inexhaustible fascination. Twisting and turning in the contortions of their skill, the glassblowers of Venice produced their goblets, their mirrors and their many-sided crystals to enhance the crimson glow of wine or multiply the refracted light of candles, while the spectacle makers of Holland, patiently and meticulously polishing, produced the optical lenses and the window-panes through which a more detailed world came into focus. But what did glass, this highly esteemed and valuable commodity, really signify in symbolic terms? Glass can be used both as a mirror and as a window-pane; it can open up new prospects and reveal a cosmos or a minute microcosm — or it can reveal us to ourselves with startling exactness, and capture a reflection even more fragile and ephemeral than it is itself. Glass therefore had an equally close connection with both the grandeur-loving and the self-deprecating aspects of baroque culture. As items of interior decoration mirrors came into their own, reaching their zenith as an integral feature in the total scheme of self-aggrandizement in the famous Hall of Mirrors at Versailles where at formal functions 400 panels of reflecting glass caught the brittle lustre of 3000 candles. Meanwhile every satirist and comic writer proclaimed that he was holding a mirror up to the world. And here and there — Rembrandt in the solitude of his studio, for instance, or Andreas Gryphius on his bed of sickness — men were also gazing steadily and deeply at themselves or their

reflections, trying to capture the fleeting expressions on their faces
or the subtlest changes in outward appearance as youth merged
imperceptibly into old age. Into their own eyes they gazed, and at
the shapes and textures of flesh and skin, trying to fathom what lay
within. Descartes, the first to formulate the principles of rational
scientific method, opined that the human soul was actually located
in the pineal gland at the base of the brain. For Gryphius, who had
studied anatomy in Holland, its physiological location was less
certain; but he was as confident of its existence and survival as he
was of the fact that, when the skin has withered and the flesh has
rotted, an empty skull is all that will remain to peer through hollow
eyes at the phantasmagoria of the world around it, until it too
crumbles into dust. For nothing earthly can last for ever, and
everything that man enjoys and values will one day vanish like an
insubstantial dream.

Incarcerated of his own volition in his palace at Prague, the
Emperor Rudolf collected curios and works of art, bred steeds he
never rode, and spent long hours in his laboratories dabbling in
alchemy and science, and casting astral horoscopes that confirmed
his fears and paralysed all action. The brooding anxiety and
introspection which his behaviour manifested was widely prevalent
at the onset of the baroque age. Even in England, still relatively
untroubled by the religious crises and political uneasiness of other
parts of Europe and enjoying the high culture of the Elizabethan
age, the mood was often one of melancholy and indecision. This is
the mood that pervades *Hamlet* (1600), emanating from its
haunted Danish castle, its open graves, and its sense of impending
madness and disaster: a world where strolling players have a vital
part to play, and introspective speeches are prompted by a jester's
skull. Hamlet is newly returned from Wittenberg, the leading
university of Protestant Germany, the town that Luther and his
followers had turned into a Protestant Rome. Shakespeare could
not have made a better choice. There, in the Germany of Dr Faust,
Kepler and the mystic cobbler Jakob Böhme (1575-1624), the
spiritual crisis which heralded the baroque in Northern Europe was
especially apparent.

Perhaps the turn of the century was partly to blame? Forebodings,
disappointed hopes, and a general stocktaking of past achievements
and future prospects — all these come to the fore at such a time,
particularly when people are ready, as they were in 1600, to attach

occult significance to portents, dates and numbers. In consequence, the seventeenth century as it progressed had to come to terms not only with the rise of mathematical science and its implications, but also with the gloom and superstition which cast a pall over the beliefs and attitudes of people as it opened. In Holland, France and England this proved relatively simple: here visible advancements in trade, wealth and social organization helped to dispel the clouds. Spain continued to enjoy a golden age. But in Italy there were clear signs of nostalgia for a greater past despite attempts to build a golden present. In Germany the situation was very different. Hardly had the light of a more sanguine era begun to dawn than the German-speaking areas of Europe were plunged into the turmoil of the Thirty Years War (1618-48). The mood of gloom persisted, and superstition, sorcery and witchcraft were rampant and universally feared. Life seemed indeed to be a martyrdom, and contemplation of the grave the fittest subject for the poet's art. Elegies and funeral orations proliferated, and frequently their authors took macabre delight in drawing a moral from the natural processes of death and decomposition. They talked of graves, and worms, and epitaphs, and seemed to feel more at home in cemeteries, charnel-houses and churches than in the gaudy world of transient things. And if among the corpses lying asleep in these dormitories of the dead, there was one whose beauty when alive had been outstanding, they were apt to heighten their grief by imagining the voluptuous transports of the maggots now feasting on it, and the ghastly ravages they were making in what had been the heavenly garden of a face.

In 1643 Jacob Balde, a South German Jesuit, produced two outstanding graveyard odes. They were in Latin, and immediately demonstrated that this revered and ancient language could be an effective medium of baroque expression, as the Jesuit dramatists had also shown. His contemporaries' admiration knew no bounds: they nicknamed him the 'German Horace', recognizing that his poems were finely wrought poetic artefacts magisterially voicing a common and obsessive theme in the mother tongue of that traditional European culture which formed the basis of education still in every European country, no matter what its religious denomination or political system. As the German Jesuit contemplated the bones of the dead in a country churchyard; as the howling tempest overhead started to die down, and the majestic raging of the ocean abated just enough for him to hear the mutmured Latin whisper, 'Man is dust and ashes, and in the midst of life we are in death', he was articulating the same view of human existence as his greatest contemporaries in other languages and in the other arts. And as he gazed at the graves tranquilly spread out before him and mused on the panic turbulence of that day when the dead will rise to hasten either to eternal bliss or to everlasting damnation, until the vividness of his daydream made him shout out to them, 'Rest! Sleep on! Don't rise before I too am dead!', it is clearly audible, too, that his voice is authentically baroque. It is the voice of an artist in words, whose vision, like that of Rubens or El Greco, encompasses both this world and another, but with a spiritual and moral urgency which only words can convey.

One of those who responded to the Jesuit's achievement was Andreas Gryphius, the German Lutheran poet whose temperament and linguistic gifts were most suited to this particular aspect of the age in which he lived. Life's anguish, man's mortality and the fragility of beauty were his usual themes; but the sombre splendour of his poetry is much more than a sum total of them. Yet unlike the great paintings of the period, its buildings or its music, his achievement is incomprehensible to those who do not know his language or are unaware of the complex structures and patterns he uses to such good effect: it is the perennial complaint of the lyric poet at home in the peculiar qualities of his own language. Something of his mood and manner is conveyed, however, by those brooding speeches in which the hero of Dryden's *Aureng-Zebe* was later to express his existential insights as he waits for death:

> Distrust, and darkness, of a future state,
> Make poor mankind so fearful of their fate.
> Death, in itself, is nothing; but we fear,
> To be we know not what, we know not where.
>
> When I consider life, 'tis all a cheat;
> Yet, fool'd with hope, men favour the deceit;
> Trust on, and think tomorrow will repay:
> Tomorrow's falser than the former day.

There is more intensity and depth in the German: the phrasing is more majestic and more sustained, the alexandrines more measured in their tread than the elegantly formulated couplets of the English dramatist. But the sequence of the argument is common to them both, and so, too, is the sensation of surveying the panorama of life from a position of lofty, almost visionary eminence, a position which makes the immediacy of the central insight all the more startling:

> I need not haste the end of life to meet;
> The precipice is just beneath my feet.

There is something truly statuesque about the attitude of both these poets. Poised high above us in their elevated diction, like the saints and prophets high up on some baroque façade, their attitudes and gestures are fixed, their control rigid. Yet this appearance of monumental dignity cannot conceal the underlying anxiety for long. They are prone to giddiness, and in constant apprehension of falling. 'A Play,' wrote Dryden in his essay *Of Dramatic Poesy*, 'to be like Nature, is to be set above it; as Statues which are plac'd on high are made greater than the life, that they may descend to the sight in their just proportion.' No apter comment was ever made on form and content in high-baroque art.

But it was not of death, perhaps, that baroque artists and writers most complained, but of time, under the fatal shadow of whose wings all things decay and wither. The century which saw the invention of the pendulum clock and the balance-spring mechanism for watches by the Dutch scientist Christiaan Huygens (1629-95) was understandably also growing more and more conscious of the passing of time — of time measured not just in years, months and days, but in minutes and indeed seconds. That particular pressure of which all modern people are perpetually aware came to seventeenth-century people as something of a shock and revelation. To carry a travelling clock or pocket watch about with you, if you were wealthy enough to own one, was the first tangible and fatal step towards that acute consciousness of fleeting time which was soon to become a dominant preoccupation of the period, and which in some of its writers and thinkers was to engender a feeling of metaphysical dread.

'Man that is born of woman hath but a short time to live,' say the Book of Job and the Order for the Burial of the Dead; 'Each moment of life is a step towards death,' realizes the emperor in the last act of Corneille's *Tite et Bérénice*. Traditionally the beating of the human heart, whose functions William Harvey had just revealed (1628), had always been regarded as one of the measures of that elusive commodity, time. Time may seem to pass more quickly as the pulse quickens; yet the heartbeat can also make it seem to drag. Poets could make of this whatever they liked. Meanwhile, in Italy, where the first description of a pulse-clock had been produced in 1625, the scientist Borelli went so far as to liken living organisms to a clock, their complex component mechanisms all moving for some reason according to their own set rhythms, speeds and intervals. Connections between the notion of time, the machinery of the body, and the passions or emotions were evident to the many prominent authors and scholars whose formal academic training had been in subjects such as medicine: men like Sir Thomas Browne in England, Descartes in France, or Gryphius in Germany. Their studies and travels had taken many of them to Huygens's own university of Leyden in Holland, generally regarded as the most advanced in the various fields of scientific research in seventeenth-century Europe. Soon the impulses emanating from the advances being made in the mechanical measurement of time merged for men like these with the wisdom of the morgue and the insights of the anatomical dissecting table, at which Gryphius demonstrated and which Rembrandt graphically recorded in his group portrait of the *Anatomists* (1632). And imperceptibly that wisdom and these insights fused with a deeper spiritual awareness instilled by diligent reading of the Scriptures and, of course, by the bitter and painful experiences of life itself. The notions of mortality and transience came to dominate the age. Paul Fleming, another German doctor-poet, expressed the new awareness of man's temporal condition in a metaphysical poem entitled *Gedanken über die Zeit* ('Thoughts on Time'):

> You live in time and yet you don't know time:
> For what is time?
> Time is what you are, and you are what time is;
> No, you are less than time — it stays when you depart. . .

To baroque eyes, ever ready to read significances into signs and portents, the hands of a clock seemed to say even more accurately than the shadow on a sundial, and even in overcast weather or at night: 'Tempus fugit!' It was therefore natural enough to suppose that the comedy of life being enacted by each of us was limited to a specific, if unknown duration measured as strictly as the unity of time in some formal, regular French tragedy. And it was equally logical that the eternity of afterlife should be imagined as a perpetuity without moments, where time, the measure of all things here below, is totally irrelevant.

Awareness of another, higher plane where, bathed in the golden light of an eternal present, true reality prevails: this all people possessed during the baroque period. However sordid their behaviour here below, however craven their actions and devious their thinking, there was for all of them, even the most opportunist and self-seeking, an ever-present consciousness that this earthly life is in itself quite insufficient. Beneath the ceilings of their grandest churches, painted with such disdain for technical and economic difficulties, it was still by no means unusual for people to meet in secret assignation, for whores and panders to ply their trade and all manner of business to be done, while dogs roamed freely, sniffing at the pillars; even in Protestant Holland they can be seen in paintings of the whitewashed interiors of churches. We would be shocked by much that commonly went on in seventeenth-century Europe, despite our tendency to think that our permissiveness and theirs have much in common. It is our attitudes that are so very different. From our imperfect world we can only look up at a sky contaminated by our own technology, a sky which opens on a universe whose space, we know, is infinitely vaster than we can imagine. But they could turn from their bewildering world and gaze aloft to see the heavens open and, if they were lucky, catch a glimpse of the eternity of celestial bliss or at least a reflection of it in paint and stucco.

'Este mundo es un cero: a solas, vale nada, juntándolo con el cielo, mucho,' wrote the Spanish moralist Gracián; 'This world is a cipher, worth nothing in itself, but worth much if joined to heaven.' His aphorism brings home the constant theme of baroque thinking.

The vanity of all earthly things, reiterated in every cultural language by poets, philosophers and preachers; the acute awareness of rapacious time for ever slipping by and ready to take with it the things of beauty which we love and value most; the tomb for ever waiting around the corner as a reminder that flesh is mortal and that man is dust: all this led not to the despair of pessimism but to an extraordinary capacity for living. Baroque man could live with disenchantment, gather rosebuds while the moment lasted, and appreciate the colourful masquerade of living. The knowledge that, like a dream, it would end put it all in perspective, enhancing life for those on whom Fortune smiled, and making it bearable for those who enjoyed neither health nor money.

> Oh! how vain a thing is man even in his best estate, while he is nothing but himself, his heart not united and fixed on God, disquieted in vain! But the soul trusting in God is prepared for all, not only for the calamities of war, pestilence, famine, poverty, or death, but in the saddest apprehensions of soul, above hope believes under hope. 'Tis the godly man alone who by this fixed consideration in God looks the grim visage of death in the face, with an unappalled mind.

So preached Archbishop Leighton, a Scottish divine much admired for his piety and learning. 'There is nothing more precious than time,' proclaimed the fashionable Jesuit preacher Bourdaloue to his Paris congregation, 'for it is the price of eternity.'

'Blessed therefore is the man that feareth the Lord: his righteousness endureth for ever': the famous words of Psalm 112, *Beatus vir*, had great resonance throughout a period when men were loth to count their blessings and were everywhere wondering what could ensure their victory over time and the inevitable mutability of all things. 'The righteous man shall never be moved,' the Psalmist told them: 'he shall be had in everlasting remembrance'; the note of stoicism was congenial, and the notion of fame outliving death was the essence of all their epitaphs. Understandably Psalm 112 was a particular favourite in the Psalter, the best-known and most influential collection of lyric poetry in Christian Europe, and in many a church musical settings of it rang out. Some of the finest were composed in Venice, a great centre for baroque religious music as well as opera. Was it significant that Monteverdi based his first setting of it, in his *Selva morale e spirituale* (1641), on his jubilantly youthful secular canzonetta *Chiome d'oro* (1619), that musical quintessence of the amorous Petrarchan conceit: lavish lovesick praise for golden hair? Was this an example of the baroque awareness of the simultaneous existence of two different planes? Much later, as the high baroque was ebbing away, that other inimitable Venetian musician, Antonio Vivaldi (1675-1741), produced his version of *Beatus vir*. Flamboyant, plangent, jubilant by turns, it is the epitome in sound and rhythm of the pride and self-abasement of baroque piety and religious fervour. Perhaps it is also symptomatic of the once-great city, Venice? The Psalmist seemed almost to have written his text with the most serene of baroque settings in mind.

The seventeenth century loved the Psalms and drew deeply on them. Another biblical book which made a profound impression on them was the Book of Job. 'Our days upon earth are a shadow,' they read. 'When I lie down, I say, When shall I arise, and the night be gone? And I am full of tossings to and fro until the dawning of the day. When I say, My bed shall comfort me, then thou scarest me with dreams, and terrifiest me through visions.' The powerful expressions of tribulation and transience in Job merged easily and naturally with that other all-pervasive image which the baroque considered to be perhaps the most fitting expression of its conception of human existence: 'Life is a dream'. To the English-speaker this image sounds very Shakespearian, and here, too, as with the image of 'All the world's a stage', Shakespeare was actually taking up a long-standing idea and anticipating what was soon to become one of the essential pieces in the mosaic of European baroque culture.

> We are such stuff
> As dreams are made on; and our little life
> Is rounded with a sleep.

The famous words are spoken by the Italian duke-magician Prospero after a mythological masque has been performed on his enchanted island in Act IV of his late play, *The Tempest* (1611). They express Shakespeare's most mature philosophy; but they are also a formulation of a notion which was simultaneously developing in other parts of baroque Europe. Less than a quarter of a century later, it was to be the central, haunting theme of one of its outstanding masterpieces, *La vida es sueño*, written by Calderón in 1636.

Calderón's play embodies so many of the disparate elements that make up the total picture of the baroque, and organizes them so subtly and imaginatively into a coordinated dramatic whole, that access to it is far from easy. But Calderón realized this too, as his presentation of the action shows. As dusk is falling, Rosaura, whose name suggests a rosy dawn, enters in disguise. Her long and tiresome search for her lost lover had led her into a maze-like landscape of fantastic rocks, deep gorges and impenetrable forest:

light and shadow enhance the mood of confused uncertainty, which yet implies some hidden symbolic meaning. We could be in one of the fantastic imaginary landscapes by Salvator Rosa (1615-73), Calderón's Neapolitan contemporary; in fact, the scene is Poland, that testing-ground for young kings in the making, as Rotrou's *Venceslas* was soon to show. Rosaura espies a rugged tower of symbolically rough-hewn stones, from inside which comes the doleful sound of some lone prisoner bewailing his miserable fate. Incarcerated in the tower is Segismundo, son of the King of Poland. From birth he has been kept there in the wilderness of nature, in a state of nature just like any wild beast; he does not know that at his birth an ominous horoscope had foretold the sinful life he was to lead. The elements had raged, the sun had gone into eclipse, and the end of the world seemed to be at hand when Segismundo was born; nothing so dreadful had been witnessed since Christ's Crucifixion. Realizing that if he allows his son to live his princely life in freedom he will wreak the foretold havoc on all around him, the king has had him brought up alone, unkempt, in solitary confinement. But now the time has come to think of the succession to the throne. Should Segismundo be deprived of all his rights simply because the fact of his existence gives grounds to fear the worst? Is this not an indictment of us all?

Then, one day, Segismundo awakes to find himself surrounded by all the splendours of a royal court. It is his father's ruse to try him out. For one brief day he rules: his rule is a disaster. Then the insubstantial pageant fades, the gorgeous palace dissolves, and the dream is over; he finds that he is back again in his solitary confinement. Yet the unaccountable experience of his dream has taught him something. Gradually it dawns on him that, whether asleep or waking, there is a fundamental, inescapable distinction between good and bad, and that, whatever the reasons for his own existence, he alone bears sole responsibility for what he does, awake or sleeping. This realization is his spiritual victory over the deceitful world, and it wins him the right to be called Prince Segismundo indeed, for that is the hidden meaning of his own name. His father acknowledges him at last, and in the final jubilant moments of the drama hands him the crown of Poland. For Segismundo has learnt the moral lesson that is central to Calderón's baroque conception of the world: life may indeed be justly likened to a dream because it is almost as brief and as fantastic, and the happiness we covet is as volatile and illusory as any dream. The simile is there for us to use in order to reach a fuller understanding of existence. But the notion that life is a dream is most emphatically no excuse for us to renounce our dignity as human beings created in God's image, or to abdicate the moral choices with which each moment of each day confronts us.

In *La vida es sueño* all ends happily as in a comedy. But it is a comedy which in true baroque fashion highlights basic human experiences and illustrates traditional themes in order to make us, as spectators, aware that there is more to them than perhaps we realize. Rosaura, who stands symbolically for us all, has at last reached the object of her spiritual quest. 'How wise he is, and how great is his understanding!' she exclaims on our behalf as Segismundo describes in graphic detail his insight into the ultimate truth behind the dreamlike appearance of life. Rosaura's vision is just a vicarious one, like ours: few are vouchsafed, like Segismundo, direct experience of life's inner meaning. But her vision is not impaired because of that, since it forms part of the totality of Calderón's drama. 'That which we see in a glass assures us that such a thing there is,' said Donne in the sermon he preached at Old St Paul's on Easter Day 1628, 'for we cannot see a dream in a glass, nor a fancy, nor a chimera.' And he went on, developing his mirror image further and echoing St Paul, 'For now we see through a glass darkly, but then face to face. So this sight of God, which our apostle says we have in a glass, is enough to assure us that a god there is. For it is a true sight of God, though it be not a perfect sight, which we have this way.' He clinched his argument with a reference to his age's greatest cultural love, the stage: 'This way our theatre, where we sit to see God, is the whole frame of nature; our medium, our glass in which we see him is the creature; and our light by which we see him is natural reason.'

Donne's words could be those of his Spanish contemporary, the playwright who became both a court poet to a Habsburg monarch and an ordained priest of the Catholic church. When Calderón made his prismatic drama open on a wild symbolic landscape, he was declaring his belief that the experiences of a dramatic figure in a natural setting can mirror spiritual truths and shed light on the meaning of existence in a way which reasonable spectators can readily understand. His entire achievement as a major baroque artist depends on the assumption that the theatre can and should be used to demonstrate that human beings can penetrate to sublime and urgent truths. But to achieve this supranatural objective required simultaneous and concerted exploitation of all the resources at his disposal: scenery, lighting, movement, language and tight-knit poetic and intellectual argumentation. *La vida es sueño*, like all Calderón's mature plays, makes full use of these. Such plays could never be just a re-creation of transitory reality; they were a symbolic representation of the real drama underlying the dreams and masquerades of life.

Despite its emphasis on the transience of things, baroque culture produced art which can attain unparalleled vitality and intensity. But this is only fully evident if one is in direct contact with it. Only in performance can its plays and operas engross our whole attention and enthrall us with their sights and sounds; yet performances are rare, and most of them take place in the imaginations of sympathetic readers or listeners to recorded music. Only when actually standing in the baroque churches of Italy, Spain or Southern Germany can one appreciate the full power of their embrace, and acknowledge the enormous claims they have to make on our senses and our intellects. The intellect recognizes that much is fake. The florid sentiments, the exaggerated poses, the far-fetched metaphors and arch conceits are often nothing more than *trompe-l'oeil* tricks and gilded, painted stucco. But the senses can sometimes, even now, still register an impact; we can still marvel at the domes and ceilings, the altarpieces and organs, those technological triumphs of countless unnamed artisans and craftsmen, which actually have the audacity to capture and reflect what we can scarcely dare to think about.

In some parts of Europe the baroque lived on well into the eighteenth century, continuing to exert strong influence on various forms of culture. In central Germany, the passions, cantatas and keyboard works of J. S. Bach (1685-1750) brought to a glorious climax the long traditions of church and secular music in Lutheran and indeed Protestant Europe at a time when Leipzig, the town in which he worked for many years, was already becoming famous as a centre of the new enlightenment associated with common sense rather than with baroque vision. Meanwhile in the Catholic south of Germany a galaxy of florid churches sprang up for no apparent reason except that the church's confidence had been restored and it had regained its spiritual and material hold on a willing peasant population. The imposing monastery of Melk, perched above the Habsburg river Danube, proclaimed the victory of the faith in architecture jubilant and triumphant. High up in the Swiss Alps, this spate of late baroque building reached another climax in the Abbey of Einsiedeln, completed in 1735. Like all great baroque works it arouses astonishment and wonder. To see this enormous building, a new and less austere Escorial surrounded and surmounted by snow-capped peaks, is an extraordinary experience; but it is even more revealing to discover that inside the Abbey Church there is a carved and painted world of shimmering white and gold which, paradoxically, seems even vaster than the natural setting of alpine scenery outside.

The late baroque of Melk and Einsiedeln would have been viewed with horror by the plain, godfearing readers of Bunyan's *Pilgrim's Progress* (1678). Yet that homely Puritan allegory of an ordinary mortal's spiritual ascent from this world of vanity and misery into the world that is to come reflects a basic similarity of outlook across a gaping cultural chasm. Surely it is significant that, like some of his contemporaries in Catholic countries, Bunyan presents his view of life 'under the similitude of a dream'; in so doing he comes much closer to the spiritual and artistic values of baroque Europe than his British admirers have liked to think. It is significant, too, that as Bunyan's dream-epic reaches its zenith, and Christian and his companion Hopeful see the goal of their quest and pilgrimage rise before them in all its supernal splendour, 'the reflection of the sun upon the city (for the city was pure gold) was so extremely glorious, that they could not as yet with open face behold it, but through an instrument made for that purpose'. With that one observation Bunyan creates a synthesis of some of the most fundamental features of the baroque, and relates the new vision of the age of optics to the mystical insights of its visionaries and the grandeur-loving vistas of its architects and artists. Is *Pilgrim's Progress* then a baroque book? At all events it was a major English contribution to Europe's last comprehensive vision of a universe not yet bereft of its divinity.

For some, the vastness of that universe was already starting to become something terrifying. The French mathematician Pascal (1623-62) talked, for the first time perhaps in cultural history, of the silence of cosmic space and the terror of infinity; and, in another of his *Pensées*, he voiced the general philosophy of his period in words which reflect the stark and uncompromising quality of the Jansenist outlook, with its deep misgivings about the role of man and about life on earth:

> We can never know with certainty or be absolutely ignorant. We are afloat upon a vast expanse, and propelled on our uncertain course from one end to the other. But wherever we seek to gain a foothold, it invariably eludes us — for all things are eternally fleeting.

For Pascal, dying in the Jansenist retreat of Port-Royal, and for the vast majority of his thinking contemporaries, this was a natural fact of the human condition, however uncongenial it might be. Yet he was equally conscious of the burning desire felt by every thoughtful person, let alone by mathematicians and mystics, to discover a sound basis on which to build a tower which would reach up to eternity. We plan, we build, 'but all our foundations crumble, and beneath us yawns the abyss.'

Perhaps Pascal, pausing to think deep, was more sceptical, more racked by divine doubt, than the majority of his baroque contemporaries who, in their various ways, found solace in the notion that life on earth is really just a dream, a fleeting moment in time, from which we shall awaken to find ourselves in the timeless dimension of eternity. The sum-total of our deserts throughout this life, the final reckoning on a day of judgement like Michelangelo had depicted with such vigour in the Sistine Chapel in Rome at the end of his career, seemed now to matter less than the questions of individual moral choice and individual action. Ours are not the years that are yet to come, nor those already over; the present moment alone is truly ours — but, if we use it rightly, we gain access to eternity and to God. This was the view expressed by the German poet Gryphius, and his intensely dramatic conception of our whole eternal future dependent on sudden, split-second choice conformed to baroque tastes in art and theatre. The plays seventeenth-century audiences loved were always concerned with conflict, choice and outcome within a strictly circumscribed duration. And, more explicitly than the paintings of the Renaissance or of the neoclassical style that was to follow later, the paintings of baroque artists were arrested moments, moments when realistic detail and symbolic meaning had a simultaneous part to play in creating a dynamic yet integrated whole: a graphic vision encompassed by its static frame or setting.

They found it hard to reconcile their preoccupation with the transient moment with art of a sustained and timeless kind such as had been produced in the great classical ages, like ancient Greece and the Italian Renaissance. But in masonry and stucco, paint and gilt they succeeded in embodying their own particular vision in a composite medium which is at one and the same time long-lasting and fragile. In music, too, as it evolved from the polyphonic refinements of the sixteenth century, there emerged a counterpart to baroque architecture and sculpture: a language of sound which, like the visual language of painting, could be understood throughout Europe and which could convey passionate emotions and affecting gestures without forfeiting the evanescent quality so highly prized by baroque artists. For, until the invention of the gramophone record, music could rightly be considered the most volatile of the arts; realized, rendered audible in performance, only to die away again in silence when the musicians stopped singing, packed their instruments and left. By the end of the seventeenth century, the very notion of the constant flight of time had been crystallized into the most characteristic musical device of a whole age — the fugue, audible equivalent of life's many-stranded, complex fleetingness, which was to reach its apogee in the theoretical keyboard *Art of Fugue* by J. S. Bach, and in the grandiose fugal sections of his B minor Mass (1733). Here the great inheritor of the Protestant tradition of devotional music brought all his imagination and craftsmanship to bear on creating a liturgical work on the most lavish scale to please the art-loving court of the Roman Catholic Elector of Saxony at Dresden. In music, as in the other arts, the religious differences which had loomed so large during much of the earlier baroque period formed no great obstacle to the fulfilment of cultural aspirations and ambitions. Bach's hymn of praise to the Almighty could accommodate itself to the traditional language and liturgy of the Roman church. Why should it not also earn him an honorarium and Saxon title: for surely he deserved one?

In the domain of literature, the baroque age produced achievements of unquestionably lasting value in drama and in the shorter lyric. Occasionally, too, there were those rare feats of the imagination, when intense dramatic qualities fuse with a love of language to paint a sequence of momentous actions in illustration of a lofty and universal theme. Of these, *Paradise Lost* is the best example.

Milton's epic poem can claim to be the supreme literary product of
the European imagination at the height or centre of the baroque
period; yet the fact that Milton is England's major seventeenth-
century poet tends to obscure his European connections and
affinities. His poetry seems to be so intimately tied up with
religious and political concerns that were essentially British. Yet
were they? The tensions he felt were also largely felt by any
Protestant artist confronted with the old traditions of Europe and
the new achievements of the Catholic countries. Like many Dutch
and Germans, like Vondel and Gryphius, the closest to him in
spirit, or like the composers Heinrich Schütz and, later, Handel,
Italy and Rome meant much to him. Vondel had to seek his Italy in
imagination; but the others actually reached it (Milton in 1638) as
did so many of their more privileged and better-off countrymen in
search of art and learning. The music-loving English poet, adept at
the Italian sonnet in Petrarchan manner, able to evoke the very
spirit of Arcadia, and as familiar with the classical authors as any
other writer of his time, soon discovered that he was quite as much
at home in baroque Europe as any other European; for, like
himself, the others who were creating its culture also belonged to
separate national traditions in their various ways. The Dutch were
Dutch and proud of it, the Germans German. Yet they shared a
common background and a similar outlook on their world and age;
in a sense they could all say with Cicero and St Paul, 'Civis Romanus
sum', for to them the resuscitation of the Roman heritage and spirit
was no mere dream. It was a glorious contemporary reality that
affected every sphere of cultural life.

   In theme and manner Milton's epic spoke for that age and for all
thinking people, provided they could read it, the particular felicity
of its language enhancing rather than limiting its relevance and
range. How significant that he avoided overt reference to sectarian,
insular issues in order to concentrate on topics which, at least by
implication, were the concern of people everywhere. Rebellion,
pride and fall, and the perils and rewards of love and wisdom: these
were themes and interests common to all the contemporary litera-
tures of Europe; they were also integral elements of Milton's cosmic
vision of the perfect state of man at the Creation, and of his
subsequent unhappy fall from that first state to the familiar
condition we like to term 'reality'. As Adam and Eve walk out into
their uncertain, solitary future,

The world was all before them, where to choose
Their place of rest, and Providence their guide.

And we perhaps now realize that Milton's vast poem of fall and loss is in a sense an inversion of Calderón's *La vida es sueño*, that symbolic dramatization of a solitary man's successful attempt to regain his lost original spiritual balance. Setting out from opposite directions and against political and social backgrounds dissimilar in many respects, the English Puritan and Catholic Spaniard have deep bonds between them, the bonds of a shared spiritual and cultural outlook.

Backed by Christian teaching and by the example of antiquity, baroque art had verbal and visual confidence enough to endow all things with significance and thus ward off the absurdity of the void. Until gradually its own bright vision, too, began to fade. By the second quarter of the eighteenth century the dust had settled on its glories and the gilt had begun to tarnish. Almost everywhere in Europe, common sense and reason pointed in new directions, and new vistas of a sober, balanced kind were opening up which promised sensible solutions to the so-called problems besetting individuals and the society in which it was their privilege and function to play a modest part. Excess became unfashionable. 'Good' taste was 'in'. Admiration, that number-one response courted by all baroque artists in every medium, seemed vulgar when compared with more rational and circumspect responses, for 'fools admire, when men of sense approve'. Placid parks, naturally graced by sheets of water, agreeable groups of trees, and houses whose chaste appearance belied their modest owners' landed wealth: these were re-creations of an earlier dream of civilized living which had arisen in various parts of Europe at the close of the Renaissance, before the full advent of the baroque itself. And along with this eighteenth-century return to the simplicity of Palladio in architecture and to the unaffected nobility of Raphael in painting (or the wistful grace of Watteau and Fragonard), there went a rejection of the baroque and all the nonsense which it stood for. In France, Boileau had written; so, too, in England had Pope, whose *Essay on Criticism* (1711) marks for the English-speaker the final reckoning with a defunct culture whose hold in any case had been precarious on many aspects of seventeenth-century English taste. Pope's every barb and diatribe in the *Essay* can be seen as an integral part of the onslaught, the very temperate but cruelly effective onslaught of neoclassicism on a way of looking at things and recording them which had become both obsolete and, for a time, ridiculous. Like all such violent changes of cultural course, it was both clearsighted and curiously obtuse. As Pope inveighed, for example, against those poets and painters who

> With gold and jewels cover ev'ry part,
> And hide with ornaments their want of art,

the one questionable link in his witty chain of argument is of course the single word 'want'. For jewel-encrusted and gilded the art and poetry of the baroque certainly was, and no one grasped its externals better than its arch-critic Pope.

From the moment that the most talented and influential critics in Europe began to turn against the artistic values of preceding generations, the culture of the baroque was doomed. Lingering vestiges of baroque influence appeared unbalanced and insane: quite literally so in the case of Christopher Smart, who was discharged uncured from an asylum and promptly wrote his masterpiece, *A Song to David* (1763), a poem which displays so many of the characteristics of baroque devotional poetry and to such fine effect that its late appearance makes it an anomaly on grounds of chronology alone. For by the time the unbalanced Smart was composing his rapturous yet strictly formal paean in praise of the Old Testament prince of lyric poets, the earliest stirrings of Romanticism were already being felt in Europe and the age of reason and neoclassicism was soundly established. By common consent a rational, enlightened and uncomplicated outlook had successfully replaced a cultural farrago having neither rhyme nor reason. Empiricism was the order of the day, not allegory and talk of other levels of transcendental meaning or *double entendre*. The scientific impulse which had played so significant a part in the formation of baroque culture continued unabated; but thinking and philosophy had changed. Mirrors were now just elegant, useful looking-glasses, while graves and tombs cast a sentimental shade which could not conceal an increasingly optimistic expectancy of life. For life was no baroque dream; and it was high time that the growing middle classes of Europe realized the fact and got on with the daily business of living.

Select bibliography

(I) The visual and spatial dimensions of the baroque are discussed and illustrated in a great many books. The following are for the most part readily accessible to English readers:

Andersen, L. *Baroque and Rococo Art*. London and New York, 1969. (A comprehensive illustrated survey translated from the German.)

Baur Heinhold, M. *Baroque Theatre*. London, 1967. (An enthralling, richly illustrated introduction to baroque stagecraft.)

Bazin, G. *The Baroque: Principles, Styles, Modes, Themes*. London and Greenwich, Conn., 1968. (A stimulating and perceptive study translated from the French.)

—— *Baroque and Rococo*. London, 1964. (Attractive for its many colour illustrations.)

Busch, H., and Lohse, B. *Baukunst des Barock in Europa*. Frankfurt, 1961. (A copiously illustrated account of baroque architecture in Europe.)

Hager, W. *Baroque Sculpture*. London, 1964. (With fine photographic reproductions.)

Hausenstein, W. *Vom Genie des Barock*. Munich, 1962. (A classic of German highbrow criticism originally published in 1920 and reprinted with fine illustrations.)

Hempel, E. *Baroque Art and Architecture in Central Europe*. Pelican History of Art Z 22. London, 1965. (Very well illustrated.)

Huyghe, R. *Larousse Encyclopedia of Renaissance and Baroque Art.* London and New York, 1964 (1974). (A wide-ranging survey conducted from a French point of view.)

Kitson, M. *The Age of Baroque.* London, 1966. (A useful survey wider in chronological range than its title suggests.)

Kubler, G., and Soria, M. *Art and Architecture in Spain and Portugal and their American Dominions 1500-1800.* Pelican History of Art Z 17. London, 1959. (An authoritative survey.)

Lees-Milne, J. *Baroque in Spain and Portugal.* London, 1960. (Contains much evocative detail and some unusual illustrations.)

Martin, J. R. *Baroque.* London, 1977. (An impressive and up-to-date account from the art historian's point of view.)

Nash, J. M. *The Age of Rembrandt and Vermeer. Dutch Painting in the Seventeenth Century.* London, 1972. (A rich collection of more or less relevant visual images.)

Pinder, W. *Deutscher Barock.* 'Die blauen Bücher', rev. ed. 1961. (The authoritative photographic guide to baroque architecture in Germany.)

Sewter, A. C. *Baroque and Rococo Art.* London, 1967. (A sensitive exploration of baroque on location.)

Stamm, R. *Die Kunstformen des Barockzeitalters.* Berne, 1956. (An anthology of 14 lectures by German scholars and art historians on the formal aspects of baroque art and architecture: without illustrations.)

Tapié, V.-L. *The Age of Grandeur. Baroque Art and Architecture.* New York, 1960. (A translation of Tapié's distinguished 1957 study, *Baroque et classicisme.*)

Waterhouse, E. *Italian Baroque Painting.* London, rev. ed. 1969. (An authoritative account of the subject.)

Wittkower, R. *Art and Architecture in Italy 1600-1750.* Pelican History of Art Z 16. London, 1958. (An authoritative account of the subject.)

(II) Broader background aspects of the baroque are provided by:

Stoye, J. *Europe Unfolding 1648-1688.* London, 1969. (In the Fontana History of Europe series, this represents a masterly survey of the period from the historian's point of view, with suggestions for further historical reading.)

Friedrich, C. J. *The Age of the Baroque 1610-1660.* New York, 1952. (A notable attempt to link cultural and historical events.)

Coles, P. *The Ottoman Impact on Europe*. London, 1968. (Focuses attention on the Turkish aspect.)

Angyal, A. *Die slawische Barockwelt*. Leipzig, 1961. (Though written in German and very erudite, deserves mention because it reminds Western readers of the Slav contribution to seventeenth-century culture.)

Hook, J. *The Baroque Age in England*. London, 1976. (Attempts to come to terms with this vexed and neglected aspect of British cultural history.)

Falkus, C. *The Life and Times of Charles II*. London, 1972. (Concentrates on the period as experienced in Britain.)

Hall, A. R. *From Galileo to Newton 1630-1720*. London, 1963.

Wolf, A. *A History of Science and Technology in the 16th and 17th Centuries*. New York and London, 1935. 3rd ed. 1962. (Both trace the thinking and consider the discoveries that were being made in every field of pure and applied science during the baroque period.)

Robertson, A., and Stevens, D. *Renaissance and Baroque*. Pelican History of Music, 2. London, 1963. (Does much the same for music.)

More localized information about the period's music is provided by:

Antony, J. R. *French Baroque Music*. London, 1973.

Bukofzer, M. F. *Music in the Baroque Era*. London, 1948.

Testi, F. *La musica italiana nel seicento*. 2 vols. Milan, 1972.

(III) The literary aspects of the baroque receive particularly perceptive or original treatment in a number of books:

Warnke, F. J. *Versions of Baroque. European Literature in the Seventeenth Century*. New Haven, Conn., and London, 1972. (The most ambitious and cosmopolitan study of baroque literature available in English: a literary counterpart to J. R. Martin's recent volume of art history.)

Petersson, R. T. *The Art of Ecstasy. Teresa, Bernini and Crashaw*. London, 1970. (An outstanding and sophisticated essay in baroque culture.)

Martz, L. *The Wit of Love*. Notre Dame, 1969. (A 'baroque' approach to four seventeenth-century English poets.)

—— *The Poetry of Meditation*. New Haven, Conn., 1954. (A

probing inquiry into the workings of religious and mystical verse.)

Mirollo, J. *The Poet of the Marvelous.* New York, 1963. (An introduction to Giambattista Marino and thus to European high-baroque poetry in general.)

Hill, J. P., and Caracciolo-Trejo, E. *Baroque Poetry.* London and Totowa, NJ, 1975. (An invaluable and well-selected anthology of poems in their original languages with introductions and translations into English.)

Cohen, J. M. *The Baroque Lyric.* London, 1963. (Can be read in conjunction with the anthology.)

Greg, W. W. *Pastoral Poetry and Pastoral Drama.* London, 1906. (An epoch-making and authoritative study.)

Loftis, J. *The 'Revels' History of Drama in English.* Volume V: 1660-1750. London, 1976. (The most recent account of the stage in 'baroque' England.)

Wilson, M. *Spanish Drama of the Golden Age.* London, 1969. (A useful introduction to Calderón and others.)

Gillespie, G. E. P. *Daniel Casper von Lohenstein's Historical Tragedies.* Columbus, 1965. (Provides an excellent introduction to this writer for English readers.)

Smit, W. A. P., and Brachin, P. *Vondel.* Paris, 1964. (In French: a valuable introduction to the life and works of Holland's greatest baroque writer.)

Rousset, J. *La Littérature de l'âge baroque en France: Circé et le paon.* Paris, 1954. (One of the undisputed classics of modern baroque criticism.)

Tapié, V.-L. *Le Baroque.* Que sais-je? No. 923. Paris, 1974. (Attempts to define the baroque in broad cultural terms.)

Rosa, A. A. *Il Seicento.* La letteratura italiana; storia e testi, Vol. V. Rome, 1974. (An anthology of Italian texts relating to the baroque period, with useful commentary.)

Orozco Díaz, E. *El teatro y la teatralidad del Barroco.* Barcelona, 1969. (A penetrating study of the pervasive theatricality of baroque culture from the Spanish point of view.)

_____ *Manierismo y Barocco.* Salamanca, 1970.

Barner, W. *Der literarische Barockbegriff.* Darmstadt, 1975. (Much has been written in German on baroque literature. This valuable compendium contains numerous critical evaluations of the subject, from Wölfflin (1888) to the present day.)

Index

Page references in italics refer to main entries.